# SYMBOLS

# SYMBOLS

## SANDRA FORTY

METRO BOOKS
NEW YORK

©2008 by Salamander Books

This 2008 edition published by Metro Books,
by arrangement with Salamander Books,
an imprint of Anova Books Group Limited.

Anova Books Group Limited,
10 Southcombe Street, London,
W14 0RA, U.K.

Metro Books
122 Fifth Avenue
New York, NY 10011

ISBN-13: 978-1-4351-0915-5

Printed and bound in Malaysia

1   3   5   7   9   10   8   6   4   2

# Contents

|  | Introduction | 6 |
| Chapter 1 | Egypt and the Middle East | 10 |
| Chapter 2 | African Symbols | 38 |
| Chapter 3 | Eastern Symbols | 53 |
| Chapter 4 | Early Culture Symbols | 69 |
| Chapter 5 | Astrology, Mysticism, and Myth | 80 |
| Chapter 6 | Religious Symbols | 108 |
| Chapter 7 | Politics and Power | 125 |
| Chapter 8 | Symbols from the Western Tradition | 133 |
| Chapter 9 | American Symbols | 165 |
| Chapter 10 | Scientific and Mathematical Symbols | 192 |
| Chapter 11 | Modern Information Symbols | 237 |
|  | Bibliography | 253 |
|  | Index | 254 |

# INTRODUCTION

Visual keys are extremely important in the modern world, where there is so much competition for our attention, our money, and our loyalty. Advertising is dominated by brands, which are marketed with a symbol that stands for the product—the auto industry provides many examples of this. The manufacturer's mark can represent a whole lifestyle; it stands for a a set of qualities that the manufacturer would have us associate with their product, reinforced by advertising and branding.

There are many examples of brand identity in our consumer society—from designer clothing labels to food products. All the attributes of a product can be summed up in one logo or symbol because time (and, often, a lot of money) has vested the symbols with these properties—and that makes them classic symbols.

The word *symbol* comes from the Greek word *symbolon,* a graphic sign for an idea, concept, or object. The first symbols evolved as prehistoric man learned to make marks with charcoal. Our ancient ancestors depicted their hunts, their prey, and themselves on the walls of their caves. It is likely that these images were part of primitive nature worship and were symbolic of their wish for success in the hunt.

Universal concepts were conveyed in symbol form by ancient societies around the world: all cultures have symbols for what were seen as the five basic elements—fire, water, earth, sun, and wind. In ancient worship the elements slowly took on human nature and moods, and in time became personified in the form of gods and goddesses. Indeed, many symbols stood for a deity or cult object to such a degree that the very symbols themselves became objects of worship. As the pantheon of gods grew, the original symbols were rarely abandoned:

instead they were incorporated into the costume or aspect of a particular god. In this way the link with the past philosophy was retained and merged with the new as complex ideas grew and developed.

Within ancient cultures or societies, symbolic attributions and associations were well known and understood. But we have lost the meanings of many of these, and today interpretation of ancient symbols can be extremely difficult. Often we have to grapple with concepts that, within the scope of our modern knowledge, seem to have no relevance or basis in fact—such as the ancient Egyptian interpretation of the sky as a cow.

In our everyday lives, symbols function as signposts; they are glimpsed at and understood on an almost subconscious level. They can supply instant information without an intermediary like a priest or judge. Symbols have always been useful to religious groups, particularly when followers were unable to read the texts for themselves. In fact, our ancestors were extremely skilled at interpreting symbols; in less literate times this substituted for reading skills.

Today we use words as well as associated symbols; symbols are as relevant as words in our society—they are quickly recognized and they are useful in bridging language barriers.

The link between language and symbols is strong. Some of the very earliest scripts were made up of pictograms—pictorial symbols of an object or action—rather than a combination of letters. Pictogram writing systems tended to be developed by hunting and farming cultures; the earliest were in Sumer, Egypt, and China. Despite their apparent simplicity of function, pictograms can convey remarkably complex ideas and, in context, specific information. Examples of such writing include the hieroglyphics of ancient Egyptians and those developed by Native Americans in North America.

The next symbol development was the devising of word signs, or logograms, to be used alongside pictograms to provide more specific information. The ancient Egyptians and Chinese successfully combined the two methods in later dynasties. But hieroglyphs remained virtually unchanged for centuries, perhaps as a reflection of the almost static Egyptian society itself.

All modern societies make use of myriad symbols to convey information at a glance. Consider how many you see in a single day and how much information you

absorb without even noticing. This is especially true in cities; not only is a vast amount of directional and safety information conveyed through the use of symbols, but also a huge amount of general information about all the things we see. In our fast-paced lives, symbols save time and thought.

As a result of this unconscious recognition factor, symbols are often used to reinforce messages. They are often incorporated by designers, architects, and craftsmen as decoration and embellishment; public buildings often include allusions to their purpose or founding ethos: courthouses show the figure of Justice; cathedrals show images of Christ; hospitals display the rod of Aesculapius; palaces display symbols of victory and power; and agricultural halls incorporate wheat sheaves and cornucopia. Grand private houses can display ornamental symbols to reveal the foundation of the fortune, the profession, or personal interests of their owners. The use of symbols is taken further when incorporated into medals, jewelry, clothing, furniture, and the majority of man-made objects. They can be worked into patterns and motifs, and are sometimes

redrawn or distorted until only an expert eye can discern their presence.

Symbols function at many levels. Many have significance in only one country or culture, and the same symbol can have entirely opposite meanings in different places—for example, a dragon in China is a positive symbol of good fortune, but in Western cultures a dragon often symbolizes evil, danger, and destruction. Symbols reflect the beliefs and social customs of their time and culture. In many instances they have been transferred through trade, conquest, and cultural (often religious) links to nearby societies to become incorporated by an entirely different civilization. Thus deities transmute and, confusingly, can sometimes acquire completely contrary aspects. For example, the Mesopotamian goddess Ishtar was named Inanna in Sumer and Astarte in Egypt. Under these and other regional names she was popularly worshiped as the goddess of love and fertility, but she was also feared and invoked as the terrifying goddess of war. Many symbols are associated with the worship of deities through an intermediary animal or elemental form. As such they are recognizable by their symbolic clothes, headgear, decorations, and attributes.

Many symbols can be international in their meaning; the prime example of this is the drawing of a heart to symbolize love. More modern examples include those that provide an international language—such as scientific symbols or those linked to the use of the Internet, like the @ symbol. National flags and other heraldic devices are obvious universal symbols whose original use may have been to identify friend from foe on the battlefield but over time took on more universal meanings and significance.

While most symbols are overt, designed to disseminate information to as many people as possible, there are also many that have another, covert function to convey information clandestinely to people within a special group. Such methods of communication were—and still are—used extensively by religious and political groups. Early Christians, struggling from persecution, signaled to each other using a variety of symbols, the best known of which was the fish sign. American migratory workers and homeless vagabonds once had a secret code that conveyed to those "in the know" information about food, shelter, or danger. Disregarded, ignored, or just not seen by the general public, covert symbols can be publicly displayed and reveal information only to initiates—it is not a great jump from symbols to codes and ciphers.

The majority of symbols are benign, with straightforward connotations. But like the swastika—an extremely old sign perverted in the past century—they can also become associated with evil. The use of symbols by extreme religious or political factions take on the opprobrium that ordinary people feel. The cross may be a symbol of faith to the Western world, but it has connotations of the merciless Crusades to others; the hammer and sickle was not a benign symbol to the free world at the time of the cold war.

This book will introduce you to the fascinating world of symbols and convey something of the ideas and philosophies attached to a range of symbols from around the world. The book is divided into chapters by topic, and within each chapter there are sections—these sections are denoted by a change in the color-coded line. Every culture, religion, political philosophy, and hierarchy has employed symbols. They are as relevant to our lives today as they were to our distant ancestors. Symbols provide a pathway to the thought processes and cultures of the past.

# Egypt and the Middle East

Ancient Egyptian is one of the oldest recorded languages in the world and has the longest documented history of any language. It was in continual use for about 4,000 years. The meanings of hieroglyphs were lost until the early nineteenth century, when a young Frenchman, Jean-Francois Champollion, began unraveling them.

Ancient Egyptian culture relied heavily on symbols that were interwoven with their complex mystical, solar, regal, and astrological beliefs. The most obvious representation was in their writing, in which script and image were one and the same.

Hieroglyphs are composed of three basic types. *Ideograms* are symbols that are literal representations of ideas and have no phonetic value—for example, a drawing of a house for "house." *Phonograms* represent sounds of the language and provide the aural basis for a word—for example, a drawing of a beetle for "B." *Determinatives* are placed at the end of a word to show its category and have no phonetic value, like the plural indicator; they are important because they show the reader what word he is looking for when there are only consonants to read.

The hieroglyphs for the gods are true symbols: a throne for Isis, a falcon for Horus, and a jackal on a shrine (naos) for Anubis. Some are derived from analogy: the word for green and prosperity was shown by the symbol of a papyrus; the word for red and blood was symbolized by a flamingo.

Another way of telling which god is referred to is to look at the headdress, which was an important detail of their appearance. Horus, for example, wore a double crown, and Nefertem a lotus flower. But this is not a foolproof system; when a god's mood or aspect changed the emblems changed to take on another's aspect. To make matters more confusing, some gods and goddesses shared the same headdress.

### All-seeing eye (in pyramid)

An ancient Egyptian symbol indicating that the dead god is entombed in the underworld but is still watchful during his period of incarceration before his rebirth. The open eye is his soul that is still alive, so he knows what is happening in the world. This symbol is seen by millions of Americans every day: it appears on the back of the one-dollar bill as well as on the Great Seal of the United States. The symbol is also used by the Freemasons, an association that attracted the designers of the bills and the seal.

### Ankh

This symbol may originally have been taken from an ankle strap. As a hieroglyph it means "life" and as a symbol it is a sign of the vital elements air and water. Egyptian gods are often depicted presenting an ankh under the nose of a pharaoh—symbolically giving him the "breath of life." The ankh shows the imperishable, vital force of life. Sometimes ankhs are shown representing a stream of water flowing over the pharaoh's feet during ritual purification.

### Book, writing, abstract thought

The hieroglyph for book, writing, or abstract thought is represented by the symbol of a scroll. Books as know we them today did not exist in ancient Egyptian times— instead, papyrus reeds were formed into a kind of paper, and then rolled up and secured with a cord. All kinds of information would have been recorded on scrolls, · including plans for buildings, records of harvests, and astronomical observations. Abstract thought and writing were new concepts in ancient times, and due to the conceptual similarities between them, they used the same symbol.

Egypt and the Middle East

### Desert, foreign country

The hieroglyph for desert or foreign country represents flowing sand dunes; to the south and west of the ancient Egyptian empire lay the vast deserts of the Sahara and beyond. To the east lay the inhospitable deserts of the countries known today as Syria and Jordan. The term "sand-sea" is sometimes used to describe such empty, arid places, and the wave form of the desert symbol also captures this idea.

### Eat, drink, speak

The hieroglyph for eat, drink, or speak shows the kneeling symbol of a man with one hand to his face. This is a general symbol, and signifies that the action he is performing has something to do with his mouth. It was up to the reader to interpret from the meanings of the adjacent symbols what this action was.

### Eye of Horus

Also known as the Wadjet-eye, this symbol was worn as an amulet in ancient Egypt. It symbolized the power of the god of light and was a symbol of protection. The god Horus was believed to have the Sun and the Moon as his eyes; the "Eye of Horus" refers to his left eye. In Egyptian myth, the Eye battled against the enemies of light in the form of fire and was lost in battle against the god Seth. When it was retrieved by Thoth, Horus presented the Eye to his father, Osiris, to help him attain new life. In later Egyptian mythology the lotus god, Nefertum, was often shown presenting food and drink to the gods with the Eye of Horus in his other hand.

### Force, effort

The hieroglyph for force or effort shows a man wielding a two-handed tool—this could represent many things, including a hoe for working the fields, a pick for building roads, an ax for felling trees, or an adze for shaping timber. Since all such labors require seemingly never-ending hard work, this symbol is an appropriate one. The ancient Egyptians undertook many large-scale construction projects requiring lots of men working tirelessly for long periods, so this is a common hieroglyph.

### God, king

The hieroglyph for god or king depicts a human figure with a beard and a headdress. He is shown seated—he does not need to bow or kneel before anyone. The ancient Egyptians had many different gods and they played an important part in religious ceremonies and ritual performances. The creator of all things and the king of all gods was called Amun; a splendid temple was built in his honor at Karnak.

### House, building

The hieroglyph for house or building may seem a little stark, but this is the actual shape of an ancient Egyptian house. Since there was very little rain, a pitched roof was not needed, and the walls were simply made of mud held together with straw and cow dung. Houses of this form are still being built in modern Egypt, and with their thick walls they are cool inside and provide a welcome respite from the fierce heat of the sun.

### Logogram indicator

This symbol is used to denote whether a particular symbol should be interpreted as a logogram (also called an ideogram) or as a phonogram. A logogram is a symbol that represents an object—for instance, the symbol of a lion means "a lion." But a phonogram of a lion represents the sound of the first syllable, in this case "L." Only consonants were represented in hieroglyphs, and no one knows what sounds went between them, so any modern attempts to pronounce ancient Egyptian words are based on guesswork.

### Man

The hieroglyph for man shows a man kneeling on one knee—this is significant, as it shows that he is subservient and a mere mortal, since he does not sit in a chair or stand above others, as would a king or a god. He is shown without a headdress or any tools or weapons of any description for the same reasons. This also makes the symbol easier to interpret as a generalized man, rather than any particular character.

### Plural indicator

The scripts of ancient Egyptian hieroglyphs used an unusual method for depicting multiple objects. When a single item was represented in hieroglyphs, say, for instance, a duck, then the glyph of a single duck would be shown. If, however, it was necessary to show two or more ducks, then the duck symbol would be used together with the plural indicator, which simply told the reader that there was "more than one duck."

### Small, bad, weak

The hieroglyph for small, bad, or weak was represented by a small finchlike bird. It is easy to see why they considered this an appropriate symbol for small and weak, but why they considered it suitable to mean "bad" as well is not so clear. It is probable that such birds were serious pests of crops in ancient Egypt.

### Sun, light, time

The hieroglyph for sun, light, or time is simply a circle around a dot. The sun was the center of most Egyptian religions. The best-known sun god was Ra, but there were also Sekhmet, a fierce goddess of war who represented the destructive power of the sun; Bastet, a cat-headed goddess who represented the life-giving power of the sun; and Harmakhet, the god represented by the Great Sphinx. Harmakhet was the god of the rising and setting sun, which was also guarded by Aker, the double lion god.

### Town, village

The hieroglyph for town or village is composed of a circle with a diagonal cross in the middle. This signified the fact that many towns and villages were built at the site of crossroads, where markets were commonly set up on a regular or permanent basis. The creation of trading posts often drew tradesmen who then set up workshops, and before long a new village would come into being.

### Vulture

This bird lives off carrion and hangs around waiting for the weak to die, but it also serves the useful purpose of clearing away rotting meat. In ancient Egypt it was associated with funerary symbolism and its image was used extensively in tombs. In the Late Period (525–332 B.C.) the vulture came to symbolize the female principle (as opposed to the scarab as the male principle) of the universe. For Greeks and Romans, the vulture symbolized rapacious lust, a theme reprised in Renaissance painting allegory.

### Walk, run

The hieroglyph for walk or run is represented by a pair of human legs; since the symbol does not feature a torso, it is not tied to any particular type of person, and could be used in conjunction with the hieroglyph for man, woman, god, or king. Choices of transport were limited for common people in ancient Egyptian times—camels were available for the rich, or those on official business, but everyone else walked.

### Woman

The hieroglyph for woman shows a symbol similar to that for man, except that this human figure has long hair, probably the simplest way of depicting femininity in pictographic form. The woman is shown sitting down, which does not have particular significance since women did not have to show subservience to their leaders in the same way men had to.

### Wood, tree

The hieroglyph for wood or tree is, like many others, a very simple and direct one — a tree branch. Ancient Egypt didn't have a great variety of tree species, so most of the time a generalized symbol was all that was needed. Since timber had to be imported, it was very expensive and was rarely used in the construction of domestic houses. It was, however, used extensively in temples, where cost was not a consideration.

### Amentet

Amentet (also called Ament and Amenti) is the personification of the West. Her headdress is a short standard with a feather and a hawk on top. She was goddess of the netherworld, which to the Egyptians was in the west. She originated in Libya, which is symbolized by the feather in her headdress. Amentet lived in a tree next to the World Gates and offered bread and water to passing departed souls. Those who accepted became attached to the gods and could never return to earth.

### Amun

Amun is the primeval god of Thebes and is identified by the double crown of plumes (this same headdress is also later worn by Horus, who became god of all Egypt). Amun was a fertility god who symbolized the force of the wind; he was the supreme state god during the New Kingdom (1570–1070 B.C.) when he became a sun god named Amun-Re. He was a popular god with a large following. His image was used in homes to ward off evil spirits, and in Heliopolis he was the god of the morning sun and was called Re-Herakhty.

### Anhur

Also called Onuris. He is a sky god and his name means "skybearer." His symbol is a tall crown of four plumes. He is shown with one or both hands raised and is sometimes bearded and holding a spear. He was the divine huntsman—of men and animals—and also a benign but warlike god whose name was invoked against enemies who he chased away with his chariot. As Onuris he was the god of Thinis in Upper Egypt with another cult center (an area or a temple dedicated to the worship of a deity) at Sebennytus. He also symbolized the creative power of the sun.

### Anuket

Also called Anqet or Anukis, she is the wife of the god Khnum. Anuket is closely associated with the gazelle, which was worshiped in her name at Komir in Upper Egypt. Anuket is considered a gazelle in human form, as exemplified by her delicate grace, although she also occasionally appears in the guise of a gazelle. Anuket is symbolized and identified by her feathered crown. She was also known as the Mistress of the Nile; her particular cult places were around Aswan and the Nile Cataracts. Anuket is also called the "mistress of the gods" and the "lady of heaven."

### Blood of Isis

Also called the tet symbol, this was a powerful protection amulet given to the dead to symbolize the unconquerable nature of life. Ideally, the amulet was carved from a semiprecious red stone and was similar to the sacred knotted girdle worn by the gods. After the New Kingdom (1570–1070 B.C.), the tet became closely associated with the goddess Isis, and in the Book of the Dead the sign was greeted with the words "O, blood of Isis" before being presented to the deceased in the tomb.

## Double crown

Both Atum and Horus wear the double crown or *pschent* of Egypt. Atum was the creator god of Heliopolis and the personification of primeval chaos. He is always shown carrying the crux ansata—the symbol of life. Horus is the son of Isis and Osiris and is the hawk-headed solar god of Memphis. Isis raised him in the marshes of the Delta and hid him from his uncle, Seth. The pharaoh was seen by his people as a manifestation of Horus.

## Hathor

The Egyptians considered the sky to be a cow, so Hathor, the goddess of the sky, sometimes assumes bovine form, although she was also goddess of love, dance, and music. Usually Hathor is shown as a woman wearing a headdress of cow horns and a solar disk (Isis sometimes also wears this crown). She was regarded as the "solar eye" who, in ancient myth, had raised the young sun up to the heavens on her horns. She was a mother figure who gave divinity to the infant pharaoh through her milk.

## Isis

The pharaoh's symbolic mother, the embodiment of the ideal woman, and queen of heaven. Isis wears the hieroglyphic sign for "throne," a vulture headdress, or sometimes cow horns and a solar disk. She was the sister-wife of Osiris and his regent. When he was murdered and cut into fourteen pieces, she searched and eventually found all of them, reassembled him, and conceived the god Horus before embalming his body to restore him to eternal life. Her earthly role was to protect children from danger as she protected her son Horus.

### Khnum

A fertility ram figure in early period New Kingdom (1570–1070 B.C.), Khnum later became a man with a ram's head and a creator god. In his cult center of Elephantine he was the guardian of the source of the Nile who directed the annual inundation. As creator god he fashioned the gods and people on a potter's wheel and was worshiped as "father of fathers, the mother of mothers." He embodied the world and contained the sun and heaven (Re), the air (Shu), the netherworld (Osiris), and the earth (Geb): this is why he is sometimes shown with four heads.

### Khons

The god of the moon wears a moon disk and crescent on his head. His name means "traveler" and refers to his passage as the moon across the night sky. As the son of Amun and Mut, he is a sun god and appears as a young man wearing a side plait with legs bound up like a mummy and carrying the flail and crook symbols of authority. His job is to provide protection from dangerous animals. Also called Khons the Adviser, he became the god of healing.

### Lower Egypt

The symbol for Lower Egypt is the papyrus: as a headdress it was worn by Hapi, the personification of the Nile in flood (inundation). The ancient Egyptians believed that he lived in a cave near the First Cataract in which the Nile rises, so the annual inundation was called the "arrival of Hapi." Hieroglyphs show him as a naked, plump man with almost female breasts holding a bunch of papyrus and a table laden with food from which lotus flowers hang.

### Maat

The goddess Maat was the personification of the basic laws of all existence and embodied ethics—truth, law, and justice. Her headdress was an ostrich feather. The feather was a symbol of truth and judges were regarded as her priests. After death the heart of the deceased had to be assessed before being admitted to heaven. In a ceremony called the Weighing of the Heart, held in the Hall of Judgment, the heart was weighed on the scales of justice against the feather of Maat. During the weighing, the deceased read out the Negative Confession, a list of dreadful crimes and lesser sins that he or she denies. The feather can tell the truth of the confession.

### Meshkhent

The goddess of birth, Meshkhent is identified with a birthing stone or brick upon which Egyptian mothers squatted to give birth. Her headdress is a blade of grass or palm shoots, split and rolled over sideways at the ends. Egyptian women gave birth on a stool made of bricks into which it was believed that Thoth inscribed the time of the infant's death. Meshkhent would fashion the baby's *ka* (life force) while it was still in the womb and then appear at the moment of birth to announce its destiny.

### Neith

Goddess of war and domesticity, Neith is one of the older deities originally worshiped in the city of Sais. Her headdress is a shield with two crossed arrows and the red crown of Lower Egypt. She was a mortuary goddess who gave the gift of bandages and shrouds to the mummy in her role as the patroness of weaving. She is one of the four (with Isis, Nephthys, and Selket) who watch over Osiris's sarcophagus. In the New Kingdom (1570–1070 B.C.) she became a primeval deity who was neither male nor female.

### Nekhbet

Nekhbet is the vulture goddess who wears the vulture headdress (Isis and Mut also share it) or the white crown of Upper Egypt. As guardian goddess of Upper Egypt she shared protection of the pharaoh as his symbolic mother with Wadjet, the goddess of Lower Egypt. She was depicted hovering over the pharaoh in vulture shape holding a seal and a fly whisk. In the New Kingdom (1570–1070 B.C.) and Late Period (525–332 B.C.) she became a goddess of childbirth and mothers.

### Nut

Nut was the personification of the vault of heaven and her headdress was a rounded pot. She is the daughter of the air god, Shu, and sister of Geb, the earth god. She arches over the earth from east to west, touching the horizons with her hands and feet. She swallows the sun god Re in the evening and gives birth to him each morning. As such she is the mistress of all the heavenly bodies, who are her children.

### Osiris

Osiris wears the Atef crown—the crown of Upper Egypt—and a crown of double plumes with a small solar disk at the tip. Osiris is ruler of the netherworld and a symbol of resurrection. His name means "place of the eye." Osiris is the most important god in the Egyptian pantheon and appears in many aspects and disguises. His father, Geb, gave him earth to rule, which made his brother Seth very jealous. One day Seth murdered him and threw him into the Nile; the flooding of the Nile symbolizes the drowning of Osiris.

### Reshef

Reshef is the Egyptian name for an adopted deity from Assyria called Aleyin (or Amurru), who was an ancient god of war and thunder. In Egypt he wears the white crown of Upper Egypt with a central gazelle's head (although sometimes just the gazelle's horns) and a ribbon around the crown that trails down his neck. He is always pictured flourishing his weapons of war, ready to fight.

### Satis

The wife of the creator god Khnum Satis was known as the "lady of Elephantine" (a city near the First Cataract) and wore the crown of Upper Egypt with two curved antelope horns on the sides. Her job was to present water to the deceased for purification. When her husband Khnum became submerged with Re, she became the "eye of Re" and was submerged into Hathor and became a goddess of women and love.

### Sebek

Also called Suchos, his name means crocodile, and he was a god of the Nile, which flowed from his sweat. Sebek was especially revered in the Twelfth and Thirteenth Dynasties, when his acolytes worshiped him as a creator god who had appeared from the waters of chaos to lay his eggs of life on the banks of the Nile. At his cult center, at Crocodilopolis (Fayum), a live crocodile named Petesuchos was worshiped as the god incarnate and laden with gold rings and bracelets.

### Sekhmet

Sekhmet (meaning "the mighty one") was the goddess of war and battle and symbolized the rage of the sun. Her headdress is a moon disk with a serpent draped over the top (also worn by Harakte). She spread terror and accompanied the pharaoh into battle. She appears as a woman with a lion's head or as a lioness. The hot desert winds were her breath. Her knowledge of sorcery, however, made her a healer, particularly as an osteopath, and she was a loving wife to Ptah.

### Seshat

The goddess of writing and archives, and the wife of Thoth, Seshat wore a seven- or five-pointed star covered with a bow and sometimes crowned with two falcon feathers; she often wears a panther skin over her dress and carries a palm leaf. Her main function was as royal recorder, timekeeper, and auditor of royal accounts and records. She was also the "lady of builders" and her priest would draw out the ground plan of a new temple and calculate the most propitious time for laying the foundation stone.

### Upper Egypt

The symbol for Upper Egypt was the lotus, and the headdress is most often seen on the lesser god, Hapi. Upper and Lower Egypt were known as the Two Lands. Lower Egypt started where the Nile fans out to form a fertile delta and was symbolized by a uraeus (an asp or cobra), the goddess Wadjet, and the red crown (the deshret). Upper Egypt was known as the Red Land, in reference to the arid desert sands, and was symbolized by a vulture, the goddess Nekhbet, and the white crown (the hedjet).

## Wadjet

The national goddess of Lower Egypt and goddess of the Theban nome. Her headdress, a was-scepter (a forked staff surmounted by an animal head) was a symbol of well-being and happiness. It was decorated with a ribbon and feather over the sign for nome (an ancient Egyptian province, depicted by a crossed land grid showing irrigation channels). Wadjet was known as the "papyrus-colored one" and symbolized the forces of growth. Her sacred animal was the cobra, and she came to symbolize the spitting snake on the royal crown (the uraeus). In time she became known as "the eye of Re."

## Acacia

The thorny yellow flowering acacia tree is a native of Mediterranean countries, and the ancient Egyptians believed that it had supernatural healing powers. The tree symbolized both birth and death: birth because the gods were believed to have been born under the sacred acacia of the goddess Saosis, and death because the Book of the Dead states that children lead the deceased to the acacia. For Christians the acacia symbolizes immortality; it may have been used to make Jesus' crown of thorns.

## Antelope

For African desert dwellers the antelope is an important animal that symbolizes their gods. In the ancient teachings of the Kalahari Bushmen, the antelope was the first animal made by their creator god, Mantis. In southern Arabia the antelope was the symbol of the god Attar, the bringer of rain. In India antelopes drew the chariots of Soma, the Hindu moon god, and his predecessor Chandra, the moon and fertility god. Pavana, the father of Rama, and Hindu god of winds, also rides an antelope.

Egypt and the Middle East

### Assyrian sun god

This symbol denotes the supreme Assyrian deity Assur. He was the national god of Assyria and of its capital Assur, and his principal role was as god of war and protector of the state. In battle he protected his troops. In his more domestic aspect he personified the fertility of crops and animals. He is the counterpart of the older Babylonian god Marduk, whose aspects and rights he largely assumed. The symbol dates from around 850 B.C. and is found on Mesopotamian stone carvings of that era.

### Baboon

For the ancient Egyptians the baboon was the "hailer of the dawn," thanks to its frightful screeching at daybreak. They carved images of baboons with upraised hands to hail the rising sun. The baboon god, Hedj-wer, was an early form of the moon god Thoth, who was patron of scribes and lord of the divine writings (he was credited as having invented hieroglyphs). The figure of a seated baboon near a water outlet symbolizes Thoth as the god of chronology.

### Cat

Traditionally black cats symbolize the power of the moon, and because of their association with witches, evil and death. In modern times this has reversed to black cats being especially lucky. The original cat of ancient Egypt was probably a wild animal — not the domestic cat that became revered in the form of the goddess Bastet. Egyptian cats were sacred because cats are natural enemies of snakes. In the New Kingdom (1570–1070 B.C.) a male cat was the personification of the sun god, while the female cat was associated with the solar eye.

### Cedar

This huge, fragrant evergreen conifer is closely associated with the Near East and the Mediterranean and holds an important place in many cultures there. It is the national tree and symbol of Lebanon. In ancient times, cedars symbolized the hope of life beyond the grave; in ancient Mesopotamia, resin-rich cedar cones and pinecones were used in rituals to encourage fertility and to protect against harmful diseases. For Phoenicians the tree was sacred to Ashtart, the goddess of the planet Venus; and for Sumerians it was sacred to Tammuz, the god of the harvest. For Christians the cedar tree is an Old Testament symbol of Christ.

### Corn

Since the beginning of time, corn has been an important cereal for the making of bread and alcohol. It is an attribute of virtually every harvest and fertility deity. Corn deities are among the earliest worshiped gods; later deities include Demeter, Ceres, Persephone, Astarte, Adonis, Cybele, Attis, and Tammuz. For ancient Egyptians corn symbolized life-preserving powers and was depicted in funerary art. Its personification was Nepri, called "one who lives, having perished," referring to seeds sprouting and then harvest. Sometimes a mud image of the deceased was sown with seeds and left in the tomb to show the unconquerable nature of life.

### Cow

The ancient Egyptians thought of the sky as a cow, so the queen of heaven, Hathor, assumed the form of a cow and her sacred animals were called Zentet-cows. The cow itself symbolized the hope for continued existence after death. According to the Book of the Dead, seven cows and a bull were required to provide food for the afterlife. The cow was also sacred to the goddess Isis, the symbolic mother of the pharaoh, and in ancient myth the pharaoh was the son of the "great wild cow" who suckled him as a baby.

### Crescent

The crescent is an important symbol of Islam and is symbolic of divinity and sovereignty. The crescent is also an ancient symbol of the moon and an attribute of Diana, the Roman goddess of the moon. It is a symbol of the Great Mother, the lunar Queen of Heaven, and is an attribute of all moon goddesses. For the ancient Egyptian the crescent was the sign for Isis, Queen of Heaven, and for Hathor, goddess of the sky. For the Celts two crescents back to back symbolized immortality.

### Crocodile

In all cultures the crocodile is a powerful, threatening animal possessing fearsome strength. It symbolizes the devouring of souls: to be eaten by a crocodile is to pass into hell. The Greeks thought crocodiles were tongueless and therefore to them they symbolized silence. The ancient Egyptians had several crocodile cults, and their crocodile god Khenty-Khet transformed in time into Horus, the divine hunter. In the Egyptian underworld crocodiles tormented the dead, and in the Hall of Judgment the crocodile-headed monster was called the "devourer of hearts."

### Cypress

Associated with tombs and graveyards across the Mediterranean, Near and Far East, India, and China, the long-lived evergreen cypress is a symbol of immortality and life beyond the grave. Its resin was supposed to keep the body from decay but the tree itself would die if cut down. In ancient Phoenicia the cypress was sacred to the beautiful goddess of love, Ashtart, and symbolized her fertility and resurrection. The Japanese worshiped cypress trees as the dwelling places of the gods.

### Date palm

This tree was important in ancient Egyptian culture. The goddess Hathor was called the "lady of the date palm" and she (or the sky goddess Nut) gave food and drink to the dead from a palm tree. The crown of the date palm was sacred to the sun god Re, and he was believed to manifest himself high up in its crown of fronds. The fruit of the palm—dates—were a symbol of fertility in both Egypt and Mesopotamia. In many Near Eastern myths, the "tree of life" was a date palm.

### Eastern star

"Eastern star" is another name for the morning star or Venus. As the first star to appear each day, it is the one most often depicted in symbol. In the Middle East, the planet Venus, as the morning star, was a male god, but as the evening star became a goddess. In Assyria and Babylon these two deities merged into a single deity who was female—Inanna or Ishtar—but aggressive in a masculine way, so it was not incompatible with being a goddess of war. Thus Ishtar could be the goddess of love but also of bloodshed and war.

### Falcon

The falcon is a solar symbol of ascent, aspiration, freedom, and victory. An especially important symbol for the ancient Egyptians, the falcon as king of the air and king of the birds is sacred to the king of the gods, Horus, and as such is a symbol of divine kingship. Horus frequently appears as a falcon or wearing a falcon head that symbolizes his all-seeing powers. Odin, the chief Norse god, would often travel down to earth as a falcon.

### Flail

An Egyptian flail was a short rod at the end of which were two or three strips. It probably originated as a shepherd's whip, although it may have been a fly whisk. It became a symbol of pharaohic authority and of supreme power and an attribute (along with the crook) of Osiris, the ruler of the netherworld and judge of the dead. It was also carried by Min, the god of fertility.

### Fly

Because they carry disease, feed on dung, and are associated with decay, flies are a symbol for corruption. They are often presented as the earthly representatives of evil gods or as demons. For the Phoenicians, Lord of the Flies was another name for Beelzebub, the demonic agent of destruction and putrefaction. However, in ancient Egypt, the fly was believed to have magical powers of observation. It was also a symbol of bravery, due to its persistence, and honored Egyptian soldiers were rewarded with a golden fly.

### Frog

For ancient Egyptians the frog symbolized the primal forces of nature that brought the earth into being, and frog-headed statues represent primeval gods at Hermopolis. The frog was the sacred animal for Heket, the goddess of birth, and images of frogs were sometimes placed on newborn babies to protect them from evil. The green frog of the Nile came to symbolize fertility and the abundance of new life. In Late Period Egypt (525–332 B.C.), the frog became a symbol of rebirth, which possibly led to its similar meaning for early Christians.

### Hippopotamus

An ancient Egyptian symbol of bounty, protection, and female fertility as manifested in the goddess Taweret, who wore a hippopotamus head. Her main role was to help women through the traumas of childbirth. In some stories, Seth, the lord of the desert, appears as a hippopotamus and is killed by Horus. An Old Kingdom (2686–2181 B.C.) festival commemorated this event with the pharaoh slaughtering a white hippo. The hippo is sometimes thought to be the Behemoth: the great beast that God asks Job to admire in the Old Testament.

### Lamp

In ancient Assyria, the oil lamp contains the fire god Nusku (also called Gibil), who is personified in the sacred fire. The lamp sat prominently on the altar. Nusku was the governor of both gods and men: his particular task was to sit in judgment of dead souls who in life had been unfair judges themselves. Many ancient cultures buried a lamp with their dead so they could use it to find their way in the afterlife, and many religions use lamps as part of their worship to symbolize their beliefs as being the way to enlightenment.

### Lotus

This beautiful water flower was a favorite symbol of many ancient Middle Eastern and Asian cultures; they revered it as a symbol of the sun, because it opens and closes with daylight. The ancient Egyptians worshipped it as a symbol of fertility and regeneration, using it frequently on their buildings and monuments. It became closely associated with the Egyptian cult of the dead; they believed that the soul of the departed entered the center of the lotus, and funeral guests were presented with bouquets of lotus in commemoration.

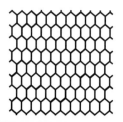  

### Net

Many gods are shown holding a net, symbolizing their power to bind and overcome their enemies. Ningirsu, the Sumerian god of the city-state Lagash and god of irrigation and fecundity, catches his human enemies with a net. In Roman mythology, the blacksmith of the gods, Vulcan, forges his own net to catch his wife Venus with her lover Mars. Nets are important in Christian symbolism, and refer to the first disciples such as St. Peter and St. Andrew who were fishermen and became "fishers of men."

### Obelisk

The obelisk originally was an Egyptian sacred stone dating from the Middle Kingdom (2040–1782 B.C.) and was the symbol of Amun, the sun god of Heliopolis. Obelisks were worshiped under the name "benben" as the first objects to be touched by the rays of the rising sun when Amun made his first appearance. They were also believed to be his dwelling place. They were usually placed in pairs at temple entrances with their four sides covered with hieroglyphs, at first for decorative reasons and then as symbols of solar and lunar deities.

### Octogram

This eight-pointed star is symbolic of the planet Venus, which was sacred to the Sumerian goddess of love and war, Inanna (also known as Ishtar). In legend, Inanna descended into hell to rescue her lover from the Queen of the Underworld (who was also her sister) and in the process passed through the seven gates of hell. These in turn became associated with the dance of the seven veils. Her acolyte priestesses were sacred prostitutes, so Inanna became known as the Whore of Babylon.

### Palm

This instantly recognizable tree is indigenous to hot climates and has significance in the culture of many lands. The ancient Egyptians revered the date palm from the very earliest times: it was sacred to the goddess Hathor and the god Re, and symbolic of fertility and good harvest. To Assyrians the palm was the Tree of Life, and in the classical world, palm fronds were used to symbolize victory. After Christ was serenaded with palms on entering Jerusalem, the palm came to symbolize pilgrims and pilgrimages.

### Papyrus

For the ancient Egyptians the papyrus was a symbol of the creation of the world from the primeval waters. The papyrus plant is a tall reed that grows along the banks of the Nile River. It was the heraldic plant of Lower Egypt and was dedicated to the goddess of Lower Egypt, Wadjet; it is often portrayed as her scepter. The Egyptian ideogram for papyrus meant "green," so the plant was a symbol for abundance and good growth. Entire stems of papyrus were presented to the gods and to the dead as the symbol for triumph and joy.

### Phoenix

This mythical bird is a symbol of immortality, resurrection, and also loneliness, as only one phoenix can exist at a time. It lives for hundreds of years until, when it feels death approaching, it builds a nest of aromatic woods, sets it alight, and dies in the flames. But from the ashes arises a beautiful, young, powerful bird. It embalms its predecessor's ashes in an egg of myrrh, and then flies with it to Heliopolis, the city of the sun, where he puts it on the altar of the sun god.

### Pomegranate

The pomegranate is a symbol of Ashtart, the Assyrian great goddess, and later of Aphrodite, the Greek goddess of love. The pomegranate contains hundreds of seeds and so was a popular symbol of fecundity and fertility, both in China and the West. For Christians it is a symbol of the church, with the red juice representing the blood of Christ and the flesh his body. It also represents chastity, because of the way the seeds are closely contained within the flesh.

### Scarab

This small beetle was revered by the ancient Egyptians as a sacred symbol of sun, life, and regeneration. It was believed that the beetle came to life from a ball of dung (the beetles laid their eggs in balls of dung to protect them). The ancient Egyptians worshiped the dung beetle as Khephri, "he who came forth from the earth." Other Mediterranean cultures later used the scarab as a symbol of good fortune.

### Shamash

Shamash was an ancient Mesopotamian solar god in the Euphrates-Tigris region around 1000 B.C. The Sumerians called him Utu, and this solar disk shows him in nonfigurate form. His symbol is a solar disk of a four- or five-pointed star with four flames issuing from the sides. He was an all-seeing, powerful deity who represented the sun and supervised man's moral conduct on earth, and as such he was Marduk (lord) of justice and judge of both heaven and earth. His special concern was the protection of the poor. At night he became judge of the dead.

### Solar barque

The ancient Egyptians used Nile boats, or barques, for cult purposes. Called solar barques, they carried heavenly bodies across the waters of the heavens. There were two solar barques that "gleamed of gold" and together symbolized the eyes of the lord of heaven. At night the left eye and moon was Mesektet, who traveled through the land of the dead and darkness to appear in the east as the day barque, Mandet, symbolizing the right eye and the sun.

### Sphinx

The Egyptian sphinx was almost always a male and a benevolent guardian, unlike the Greek sphinx that was female and always malevolent. For the ancient Egyptians the sphinx had the body of a recumbent lion with the head of a pharaoh and was a royal and religious symbol. The ancient Greek sphinx had a lion's recumbent body but the head and breasts of a woman: it was symbolic of enigmatic wisdom. Sometimes the Greek sphinx had wings and in some cases is almost indistinguishable from the Roman harpy.

### Star of Ishtar

Ishtar was the Babylonian-Assyrian goddess of sex and fertility. She was also the deity of war whose protection and support were invoked by kings and warriors before going into battle. Her eight-pointed star symbol is the planet Venus, which she wears on her head when she is in her fertility aspect. Ishtar is descended from a prehistoric mother goddess and is closely identified with fertility rites that involve intercourse between the king and the chief priestess of Ishtar. In other, nearby cultures she was called Inanna and Astarte.

### Sun disk

This ancient Egyptian symbol represents the sun god Re. Re was believed to steer his barque across the celestial ocean every day, accompanied by his daughter, Maat (the embodiment of cosmic order), and his vizier, Thoth. The ancient Egyptians had a complex relationship with the sun, which they believed to be the visible body of the lord of heaven. There were three important symbols of the day sun: the beetle in the morning, the sun disk Re at midday, and the ram in the evening.

### Swastika

This is an ancient representation of the sun's course and rotation of the heavens; in Sanskrit it means "well-being." It is especially important in Eastern cultures as a good-luck symbol. The ancient Greeks and Etruscans used it as a symbol of revival and prosperity. Early Celtic gravestones also featured the swastika, and the Anglo-Saxons called it *fylfot,* meaning "four feet," and drew it with four legs bent at the knees.

### Sycamore

The ancient Egyptians revered the sycamore as a celestial tree and the manifestation of the sky goddess Nut who protected the dead Osiris and then would "rejuvenate his soul among her branches." In fact, the Egyptian sycamore was actually a type of fig tree *(Ficus sycamorus)* that bore fruit. Its leaves were carried as an amulet to bring good luck and prosperity. One of the oldest tree cults in Egypt was for Hathor, Lady of the Sycamore, that was located near Memphis.

## Ten-day week

The ancient Egyptians used a timekeeping system that was based on a ten-day week. The symbol for this is a circle divided up into astrological "decanates," which divide the signs of the zodiac into three parts of ten degrees, each ruled by its own planet. This system of timekeeping was widely used around the eastern Mediterranean in Asia Minor, Greece, and the Levant, until after the birth of Christ.

## Winged disk

The ancient Egyptians of the First Dynasty (3300–3060 B.C.) believed that heaven lay in the wings of a falcon that stretched over the world. When a sun disk was placed between the wings, starting in the Fifth Dynasty (2760–2611 B.C.), it became a solar symbol. This symbolism originally belonged to the god Behdet; he became submerged into and synonymous with the more important god Horus, who became closely identified with the pharaoh—so the winged disk became a royal symbol. After the New Kingdom (1570–1070 B.C.), this became a symbol of protection placed above temple doors.

## Winged lion

The Assyrians showed the lion as a winged warrior, striding out to meet and conquer his enemies. Assyrians gave the lion a human head, and the mythical beast seems to have symbolized the intellectual powers of a man with the strength of a lion and the speed of a bird—an invincible beast signifying the might of Assyria. For early Christians the winged lion is one of the four Apocalyptic beasts, and it became the symbol of St. Mark the Evangelist. The Italian city of Venice also uses the symbol of the winged lion in deference to St. Mark, the city's patron saint.

# African Symbols

The vast continent of Africa is rich in symbolism, with each tribe having its own unique symbolic culture. The best known of all is the Egyptian tradition; however, other African countries have a fascinating history of symbolism, seen as decorative motifs and used on textiles such as ceremonial dress, matrimonial wear, funeral robes, and for birthing ceremonies. One of the richest traditions comes from the West African Ashanti people, who make Adinkra cloth and live in and around the Ivory Coast and Ghana.

Ashanti children are brought up listening to the legends and stories of their kings and ancestors, and the symbols they use on their cloth often refer to these stories. The word "Adinkra" may refer to an ancient battle between the Ashanti king Nana Osei Bonsu-Panyin and Adinkera, king of Gyaman (now Ivory Coast), or may simply be an inversion of the word "dinkra," meaning "farewell to the dead." This latter idea is supported by the use of the special cloth at funerals. Adinkra cloth is carefully hand printed and was probably taken up by the Ashanti peoples from Gyaman sometime between the seventeenth and nineteenth centuries.

The cloth itself takes on further significance depending on the color of the symbols—Ashanti color symbolism mostly follows the Western tradition; white symbolizes such things as virtue, joy, and purity; blue means love, dawn, and female tenderness; green, fertility, growth, and vitality; gold, kingship, god, warmth, and fire; black, old age, melancholy, and death; gray, blame and shame; red, national anger, violence, war, and death.

## Aban

Aban—castle or palace—is the Adinkra symbol of the seat of power, strength, authority, respect for the law, legitimacy, and magnificence. The symbol commemorates a historical event: the building of a magnificent palace for the Asantehene (head of the Ashanti) in 1822. The Aban also became known as the palace of culture (before it was destroyed by the British later in the nineteenth century). Aban can also represent a fence as well as signifying security, protection, and love.

## Adinkrahene

The most important Adinkra symbol is Adinkrahene, which literally means "chief or king of Adinkra designs." This symbol represents greatness, firmness, magnanimity, charisma, and leadership. It is said to have been the founding or primary symbol for the other Adinkra symbols, and in itself symbolizes the importance of playing a leading role. It is also the primary Adinkra printing symbol.

## Adwo

This Adinkra symbol means peace, calmness, spiritual calm, and continuity. It is often used in a political context and derives from the Ashanti saying "When the king has good counselors, his reign will be peaceful." It is a popular symbol in Adinkra cloth design.

### Akoben

Akoben represents the war horn used to give the battle cry to summon warriors to the battlefield. It stands for wariness, alertness, vigilance, and the readiness to be called to arms or to fulfill one's duty or fight in a good cause. The symbol is used to represent loyalty to one's nation and the need to be ready to serve one's nation when it is threatened.

### Akokonan

This symbol represents the saying "The hen treads on her chicks but does not kill them," or in short, "the leg of a hen." The Akokonan symbol, a stylized hen's foot, symbolizes the ideal of parenthood, of being able to protect and, if necessary, punish one's child. In a wider context it is a call to nurture children but not to spoil them, or could be also understood to be showing mercy.

### Akoma

Akoma means heart in the Adinkra symbolic language. It is used to represent patience and tolerance. It can also be used to signify endurance. A popular Ashanti saying is *nya akoma,* which can be translated as "take heart" or "be patient." The heart symbol is often combined with other symbols, such as Akoma ntoso (linked hearts) or M'Akoma Tu Kofe, which translates as "my sweetheart."

### Akoma ntoso

This Adinkra symbol is a stylized representation of four hearts centrally linked and signifies understanding, sympathy, and agreement. It can also stand for a charter or agreement. It is popularly used on clothing but can also be often seen on pottery and buildings.

### Asase ye dur

Asase ye dur—translated as "power of the land"—is an Adinkra symbol representing the significance of land in Ashanti economic and political power. It stands for power, wealth, might, and authority. Although land is communally owned by the Ashanti, political and economic power flows to the groups or individuals administering it as they control an important means of production in the region. The symbol can also be understood to mean life's sustainer.

### Aya

This stylized leaf is a fern. It means "I am not afraid of you. I am independent of you." When this symbol is worn it is meant as a sign of open defiance to an oppressor or intimidator. While in modern times, Adinkra designs are chosen more for their aesthetic appeal than to offer a direct message about the wearer, in the official ceremonies the symbolism is still significant. The fern symbol was used extensively on Adinkra cloth during recent high-level, contentious political meetings between Ghana and its neighbors.

### Bin Nka Bi

Bin Nka Bi can be literally translated as "one should not bite another person." In Adinkra symbology, it represents peace and harmony, as opposed to provocation and strife. It has a supplementary meaning cautioning against provoking another person into retaliation, for they will have no reason to harm you if you do not harm them.

### Dame-dame

In the Adinkra symbology Dame-dame is the name of a board game similar to checkers, and symbolizes intelligence and ingenuity. Other attributes related to the playing of this game are also represented by this symbol, such as thinking ahead, adroitness, dexterity, critical thinking, and even sportsmanship. A related Ashanti proverb suggests that "a fool can learn to play checkers," which can mean that knowledge is accessible to all or, conversely, that it is good to play checkers with a fool.

### Dwennimmen

This symbol is popular for Ashanti weddings. It represents rams' horns and signifies a mixture of humility and strength, for in Ashanti philosophy or belief the ram is seen as a creature that can fight fiercely with an adversary yet will submit meekly to slaughter. It is a call for humility even when in a position of power. It also stands for wisdom, learning, and excellence.

### Epa

Epa in the Adinkra symbolic signs of the Ashanti people of Ghana and the Ivory Coast is an abstract representation of handcuffs. It symbolizes slavery, captivity, and oppression. It is derived from an Ashanti proverb commonly translated as "You are a slave of one whose handcuffs you wear." It can also be a symbol of equal law and justice for all. It can be found on a wide range of artifacts as well as the traditional Adinkra cloth.

### Ese Ne Tekrema

Ese Ne Tekrema can be literally translated as "the teeth and the tongue." This is the Adinkra symbol of friendship and interdependence. The teeth and the tongue are separate in the mouth and have different roles but need to work in harmony together. It is a reminder of the interdependence of mankind. It can also be used to represent the importance of raising children to be responsible and productive adults.

### Fihankra

This is the symbol of the house or compound. In the Adinkra symbolic language it is a symbol of safety, reflecting the security of the typical communal Ashanti housing compound, or *fihankra*. A fihankra has only one entrance and exit and has rooms around a central open space, totally enclosing it. The Fihankra concept also encapsulates the movement between private and public space that occurs in such a building.

African Symbols

### Fofoo

The fofoo plant is a symbol of jealousy or envy in the Adinkra symbolic language, and the symbol shows a stylized floral design. It is linked to the Ashanti saying "What the fofoo plant wants is for the Gyinantwi seeds to turn black."

### Funtunfunefu Denkyemfunefu

A stylized representation of Siamese, or conjoined, crocodiles is the Adinkra symbol Funtunfunefu Denkyemfunefu. Although the crocodiles are joined at the stomach, they are still fighting with each other over food. This symbol is a reminder that infighting and tribalism is harmful to those engaging in it. It is therefore the symbol of democracy and unity within diversity.

### Gye Nyame

Gye Nyame literally means "except for God [the Supreme Being]" in the Ashanti language. It is the nonfigurative symbol of the immortality and omnipotence or supremacy of God. Today, it is one of the most popular of Adinkra symbols and can be seen throughout Ghana in a wide variety of uses and on a wide range of artifacts. It is particularly popular for weddings, represented on ceremonial clothes.

### Hwemudua

This is the Adinkra symbol of a West African measuring stick. It represents examination, superior quality, excellence, and quality control, both in goods and human endeavors.

### Hye Wonhye

Hye Wonhye is an Adinkra symbol that can be translated as "that which cannot be burned." It stands for cleanliness and chastity, imperishability and endurance, and is a symbol of good fortune. It can also be used as symbol of forgiveness or "turning the other cheek."

### Kintinkantan

This symbol is commonly translated as "puffed up extravagance," and is the symbol of arrogance. A Kantan is a traditional Ashanti ceremonial gold necklace.

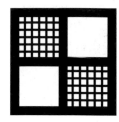

### Kolowi

This is the symbol for cowrie shells, which in themselves are a symbol for wealth. The symbol is seen on West African Mali mud cloth, called *bokolanfini* or *bogolafini* cloth. These little white shells come from a small marine gastropod (Cypraea) found in the waters off Africa. At one time these shells were especially valuable as they were used for currency in many parts of Africa and were also used to decorate clothing and various important and valuable artifacts.

### Kramo-bone amma yanhu kram-pa

This interlinked Adinkra symbol can be translated as meaning "you cannot tell a good Muslim from a bad" or "the bad Muslim makes it difficult to recognize the good Muslim." It is a symbol used to warn of the dangers of deception and hypocrisy, and suggests that deception can make it difficult to ascertain the truth. It can also be used to signify concealment.

### Kuronti Ne Akwamu

Kuronti Ne Akwamu—the council of state—represents the two complementary sides of the state in Adinkra symbolism. In Ashanti political philosophy, the head of state needs the cooperation of others to rule. It is a symbol of democracy, participatory government, the duality of the essence of life, interdependency, plurality of ideas, and complementarity.

### Mmusuyidee

Mmusuyidee can be translated as "that which removes bad luck" or "object of sacrifice." It is the Adinkra symbol for good fortune and sanctity and represents good omens and warding off evil or antagonistic powers. Ashanti legend has it that when the Ashanti king stepped on a robe decorated with this Adinkra symbol, he was rewarded with good fortune. It is commonly used to convey good wishes.

### Mpuannum

This Adinkra symbol represents five tufts of hair. This is a traditional fashionable Ashanti hairstyle, worn by royal attendants. It is derived from the Ashanti saying "One head does not constitute a jury," and symbolizes collective responsibility, justice, and democratic rule. It is a popular Adinkra design used particularly on cloth.

### Nkonsonkonson

Nkonsonkonson literally means "chain" or "link." This Adinkra symbol is a stylized representation of links in a chain. It symbolizes unity in human relationships and is a reminder of one's responsibilities to one's community, because there is strength in unified communities and man is regarded as being mutually interdependent.

 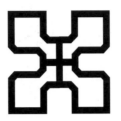 

### Nkyinkyim

This zigzag symbol is a visual representation of twisting and is used to signify initiative, dynamism, versatility, toughness, adaptability, devotion to service, and resoluteness. It is also used to stress the importance of being able to adapt or take on different roles by critically appraising and reappraising one's position in life. It is related to the Ashanti proverb "Life is full of twistings, zigzags, and ups and downs."

### Nsaa

Nsaa represents a kind of blanket. (*Nsaa* is literally a type of coarse, cloth blanket made from camel hair.) The symbol can be translated as "he who does not know the real Nsaa will buy the fake version." It stands for the recognition and rewarding of excellence, and the disregarding of the second rate or inauthentic. The symbol can be used for human relations as well as for objects.

### Nsoromma

The meaning of this starlike symbol is "child of the heavens." It is often used to describe an eminent person or a leader, or one with exceptional personal attributes. It is one of the most popular Adinkra symbols for weddings, painted on clothes or pottery. It is often linked with the symbol of the moon (Osrane) to form an additional symbol of balance, harmony, and faithfulness.

### Nyame Biribi Wo Soro

This Adinkra symbol means "God (the Supreme Being) is in his heavens." It is a reassurance that God is in his place and accessible to man. It is a symbol of hope, inspiration, and trust in power greater than oneself. The symbol is used in Ashanti architecture, traditionally on the lintel of a door—so it could be touched for good luck when passing through the doorway—as well as on Adinkra clothing.

### Nyame Nnwu Na Mawu

Nyame Nnwu Na Mawu means "God (the Supreme Being) cannot die, therefore I cannot die." It is a symbol of eternal existence. In Ashanti philosophy and belief, a man's soul is immortal; because it is part of God it lives with God after death. As with many Adinkra symbols, this one is often used in a repeated design on cloth.

### Odenkyem

Odenkyem means crocodile, and the symbol is a stylized crocodile. It is a symbol of adaptability, as the crocodile lives in the water and yet breathes air; it has the ability to adapt to different environments or circumstances. The symbol also represents propriety and prudence. It is a common symbol on decorated Ashanti swords.

### Odo Nnyew Fie Kwan

This symbol, incorporating a heart in its design, means "love will always find its way home." It represents the power of love and is a symbol of love, devotion, and faithfulness. It is a popular symbol for weddings. The heart forms the basis of many Adinkra symbols and designs.

### Ohene Adwa

Within Adinkra symbology there is a range of symbols that explicitly deals with political themes. Ohene Adwa means chief's or king's stool, as shown in stylized form in the symbol. It can also stand for Ohemmaa Adwa, the queen mother's stool, as the queen mother traditionally rules jointly with the queen. In the Ashanti political system the stool represents political authority. It is the physical representation of the philosophical construct of state territory. It stands for the authority over, or ownership of, territory.

### Osram Ne Nsromma

This Adinkra symbol combines a figurative image of a star with that of the moon. It is a symbol of faithfulness, love, harmony, benevolence, fondness, loyalty, and the feminine essence of life. It is a popular symbol for weddings, usually used on clothing or pottery utensils. It is derived from an Ashanti saying "The north pole star is always waiting in the sky for her husband, the moon."

 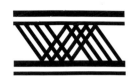 

### Osrane

Osrane is the moon in the Ashanti language and the Adinkra symbol is a stylized representation of the moon. Derived from the Ashanti proverb "It takes the moon some time to go around the nation," the symbol can represent jealousy, although it is also often joined with the starlike symbol Nsoromma to signify balance and harmony, faithfulness, and benevolence. This joint symbol, popular at weddings, can also be used to signify femininity as well as the need for interdependence and cooperation in successful relationships.

### Owo Foro Adobe

Owo Foro Adobe is an abstract representation of a snake climbing a raffia tree. The raffia tree's thorns are a dangerous challenge to the snake, so persistence and care are needed to climb it successfully. It is a symbol of prudence, steadfastness, and diligence. This symbol is sometimes translated as a snake climbing a palm tree, and has a supplementary meaning of performing the impossible or unlikely.

### Sankofa

There are several variants of this popular Adinkra symbol, which means "go back and fetch it." It can occur as an abstract motif or as a stylized bird, traditionally shown on the two-handed sword of state. It also has a supplementary meaning: that one can make good on one's past mistakes. It is a symbol of wisdom, in that one learns from the past when planning for the future: one has to recapture one's roots to move forward, or one can always undo one's mistakes. There are several figurative versions of this Adinkra symbol but they all have a similar meaning.

### Tamfo Bebre

This Adinkra symbol is literally translated as "the enemy will stew in his own juice." It represents the importance of learning from the past, or the dangers of ignoring the past.

### Tumi Te Se Kosua

Tumi Te Se Kosua is literally translated as "power is like an egg." The political philosophy represented by this symbol of a hand holding an egg is that political power is as fragile as an egg. If held too tightly it might break; if held too loosely it might fall and break. The symbol is used to advocate democracy, suggesting the virtue of sharing power. Power is not absolute and requires support and cooperation.

### Worosu

This is the mud cloth symbol for the back of a sickle handle, an essential agricultural instrument. The story goes that a farmer was so taken by his favorite sickle that he thought it deserved to be immortalized in symbol. Mud cloth can be "read" by experts using the symbols on the cloth. These are displayed in repeat patterns. This symbolism in the patterns and designs is handed down from mother to daughter, as the daughter learns the technical skill to produce the cloth. Common objects are depicted in abstract form and reproduced in design to commemorate an important event or a local hero.

# Eastern Symbols

The use of symbols in the East—particularly with regard to myths and legends—is almost as strong today as it has ever been. While each culture has its own ancient heritage, the spread of religions such as Buddhism helped to disperse imagery across nations. China and Japan have many parallels in their symbols, but it cannot be assumed that the same symbol means the same thing in each country, although it often does.

Asian art and symbols were a revelation to Western eyes when Eastern artifacts appeared in the West. Marco Polo famously brought back indications of amazing cultures and artistic traditions. The Silk Route allowed trade and the exchange of ideas, but the symbolism was almost entirely one way—East to West. Chinese dragons and birds, plants, and animals—all so distinctively different—made a huge impact on Western artists and designers. Asian motifs were incorporated into Western culture, often without an understanding of their original meanings.

As far as the West was concerned, Japan remained a mystery, due to its isolationist policies that restricted trade until the mid-nineteenth century. The barrier was broken in 1858, when America negotiated trading rights with Japan; their goods, ideas, and artistic influences took the world by storm. Japanese art and style became fashionable, but as with China, almost none of the symbolic history was known to any but the most informed connoisseurs.

India was a different story. Indians are consummate traders and their culture traveled with them. Britain established trading routes with India in the early seventeenth century and interest exploded when the British Raj was established. Much more was known about Indian symbolism in the West due to the fact that many Europeans learned Indian languages and Indians visited and sometimes settled in Europe.

### A

This is the Buddhist symbol for "A" and denotes the Supreme Lord Adi-Buddha, Vairocana. He created the other four Buddhas of Meditation—the Dhyani-Buddhas—as well as the rest of the Buddhist pantheon. He is truth and wisdom. The power of this symbol calls up the deity, and it is the first of five mystical characters that make up the Five Buddhas of Meditation. The chant is particularly characteristic of the Shingon sect of Japan. The character itself is an object of contemplation.

### Aum

Aum (or Om) is a sacred syllable that is chanted in Hindu and Buddhist prayers and mantras. It has a profusion of esoteric meanings but generally refers to eternity, infinity, or the universe. Various accounts are given of its origin; one that it is the term of assent used by the gods, and probably an old contracted form of the Sanskirt word "evam," meaning "thus." It is symbolic of creation, destruction, and preservation, or of the primary trinities of Hinduism and Buddhism.

### Bat

The Chinese believe that bats live to an old age, so they are a symbol of longevity. The word for bat, *pien-fu*, is also a homonym for "good fortune." The bat is an attribute of Fu Hsing, one of the Gods of Happiness, so it is also a symbol for joy and is often painted red, the color that represents joy. Bats are popular as motifs, and when five bats appear together they are the Five Blessings: long life, riches, ease, joy, and honors. In this aspect they are popular images on the robes of Tibetan high lamas.

### Bell

Many Eastern religions use bells as significant objects in their rituals. For Buddhists, Lamaists, Hindus, Confucians, and Taoists, the sound of a bell ringing out disperses the presence of evil spirits. The bell occasionally replaces the wheel as one of the eight lucky emblems for Buddhists. For Tantric Buddhists the bell symbolizes the universal womb and sometimes has a phallus-shaped handle. Hindus use bells to symbolize the presence of the goddesses Sarasvati and Durga. In the Orthodox and Catholic churches, the ringing of bells accompanies worship.

### Buffalo

The buffalo is sacred to Hindus, and the water buffalo is the mount of the Lord Yama, the judge of the dead. Yama was the first man to live but also the first to die. Mahisha is the buffalo demon, and he became embroiled in an epic struggle against the goddess Durga. In China one of the Eight Immortals and the legendary founder of Taoism in the sixth century, Lao-tzu, rides to the West in search of Buddhist doctrines on a black buffalo.

### Butterfly

This is a particularly popular Asian symbol. For the Japanese two butterflies symbolized conjugal happiness but a single butterfly signifies a vain woman or a hard to please mistress. In China the butterfly symbolized happiness, immortality, and endless leisure. When shown with a chrysanthemum it symbolizes beauty in old age, and when shown with a plum it symbolizes long life. For the Aztecs butterflies symbolized fire, the souls of dead warriors, and unfortunate women who died in childbirth.

### Carp

The carp is supposed to live for hundreds of years. Its persistence in returning to its spawning grounds makes it a symbol of strength and perseverance for both the Chinese *(li)* and Japanese *(koi)*. In China carp return up the Huang-Ho (Yellow River) to spawn, and when they jump through the Dragon-gate rapids they are said to be transformed into dragons, symbolizing success (especially in state exams). For the Japanese samurai caste carp symbolize martial vigor, thanks to their armor-like scales. Furthermore, their "whiskers" suggest that they possess supernatural powers.

### Cherry

*Sakura* in Japanese, cherry blossom is synonymous with Japan, where its delicate pink blossoms are the national emblem. In both China and Japan cherry blossom is a symbol of spring—the time of year it appears—and of feminine beauty, because of its delicate pink perfection. However, because cherry blossom falls quickly or is soon blown off the trees, it is also a symbol of the purity of youth and short-lived beauty. Sometimes young samurai who have been killed are alluded to as fallen cherry blossom.

### Chrysanthemum

A popular Eastern symbol in China and Japan. The Taoists in particular used the chrysanthemum to symbolize longevity on many decorative objects. The chrysanthemum in time became stylized into a sixteen-petal rosette with a central calyx called *kikumon*. The kikumon became the symbol of Japanese imperial power; the emperors wore the emblem on their robes and had it emblazoned on their ceramics. In China the chrysanthemum symbolized long life and also the season fall. In Chinese the word for chrysanthemum means "to remain."

### Cicada

This noisy insect is called *ch'an* in Chinese, and for the Chinese it is an ancient symbol of resurrection and immortality and of purity. The life cycle of a cicada starts when it is underground as a larva; it then turns into a pupa and for its final metamorphosis becomes a flying insect. In ancient Chinese funerary rites (late Chou period 1100–256 B.C. until the Han dynasty 206 B.C.–A.D. 220), a carved jade cicada was placed in the mouth of the dead to protect them in the afterlife and to ensure immortality. Its association with purity came from the belief that it fed only on dew.

### Cloud

The Chinese word for cloud is *yün,* and this is an ancient symbol of plenty—a heavenly gift brought by the rain. The dragon was revered as a rain bringer *(yün lung),* and on occasion it could be glimpsed between the clouds. The Chinese and Japanese gods also appear out of the clouds or travel on clouds from place to place. The word *yün* is almost a homonym for the word for luck, so it also symbolizes happiness and good luck and was used extensively as a decorative motif. In the Old Testament God often speaks from behind a cloud that symbolically and literally conceals his mystery.

### Club

A club is carried by many gods as a symbol of their power and also of their sexuality. The club, *gada* in Sanskrit, is an attribute of Vishnu, the Hindu god of love, and when he carries one it symbolizes his authority and the power of knowledge. A club made from a human tibia and topped by a skull is known as a *khatvanga* and is carried by many Tantric Buddhist demonic deities.

### Cock

The cock is a solar bird and usually an attribute of the sun gods. It symbolizes the dawn, courage, and vigilance. A black cock at one time was believed to be an agent of the devil, and two black cocks fighting each other are symbolic of the battle of life. For Buddhists the cock lies at the center of the Round of Existence (alongside the pig and snake) and symbolizes pride and carnal lust. For the Chinese the cock represents bravery, faithfulness, and benevolence. The white cock wards off ghosts, and the red cock was originally the sun and will protect against fire.

### Crow

Called *karasu* in Japanese. Early Taoist belief taught that a three-legged red or golden crow lived in the sun, so it is a sun symbol. A three-legged crow is the messenger of Amaterasu, the Shinto goddess of the sun; she commands the skies (the Plain of Heaven) and without her the sun will not appear. Thanks to its position as a messenger, the crow is sometimes a bird of ill omen. Crows appear on Shinto shrines belonging to the Kumano sect. Due to its odd number of legs it is a yang bird.

### Dagger

When the Hindu Mother-Goddess is in the dangerously destructive aspect of Kali, she carries a dagger. (In her positive aspect she is Durga or Parvati.) In tantric Tibetan paintings Kali is shown holding a dagger topped with peacock feathers. For Assur, the national god of the Assyrians, the dagger was a symbol of his invincible power, and in his temple the strongest oaths were sworn on his dagger.

### Dog of Fo

This Chinese mythological animal is half dog and half lion. *Fo* means Buddha, and the Dog of Fo, or lion-dog, traditionally guards Buddhist temples and images of Buddha all around the Far East. It rests a paw on the *cintamani,* the sacred jewel of Buddhism. Lion-dogs guard in pairs, a male and female; the male with the jewel and the female with a lion cub. Sometimes its dangerous nature is shown by flames spitting from its fangs; at other times, it is shown playing with a ball of silk attached to its mouth by a ribbon.

### Dragon

The dragon is important in many cultures as a combination of bird and serpent. In earliest times it was a manifestation of life-giving waters and the breath of life, and was an intermediary between the sky gods and the earthly kings. Symbolizing vital rain, the dragon also came to represent thunder, lightning, and flood, and became more malevolent. In China the dragon possesses supernatural power and symbolizes strength, hidden wisdom, power, and fertility; generally Asian dragons are forces for good, but in the West dragons are angry, destructive, and generally evil.

### Dragonfly

The islands that comprise Japan resemble the shape of a dragonfly, so Japan is sometimes called Akitsu-shima or Dragonfly Island. This short-lived but beautiful iridescent flying insect — *tombo* in Japanese — is one of the emblems of Japan. Thanks to its apparently erratic, darting flight, the dragonfly has become a symbol of instability and unpredictable behavior in both Japan and China. In the latter country, dragonflies are a symbol of summer.

### Drum

The drumbeat is important in many religious rituals—it beats the time and leads the dance. For Hindus the *damaru* (rattle drum) is an attribute of Shiva when he is Nataraja, king of the cosmic dance. When he holds the drum it signifies the creative skill of making music. Tibetan Buddhist gods use the drum when in their demonic aspects. In other religions the sound of the drum foretells the howling winds and violent earthquakes that will bring about the end of the world.

### Elephant

Elephants have more significance in Eastern and African mythology than in European and American cultures. For Hindus the elephant is an aspect of Ganesh when he is admired for his strength. Hindus also revere Airavata, the sacred white elephant who carries Indra, king of the gods. Buddhists use the elephant as a symbol of Buddha's serenity as well as of his power. For the Romans and Greeks the elephant's longevity symbolized wisdom acquired through a long life. In medieval bestiaries elephants were used as a symbol of the chastity of Adam and Eve; they also symbolize faithfulness and innocence because they mate for life.

### Fu

The Fu symbol is one of the twelve ornaments embroidered on Chinese imperial robes worn by the emperor. *Fu* is a homophone for "forbid" in Chinese and means the discernment between good and evil, so in ancient times it became the symbol for justice. It is also the Chinese symbol for the authority and divine power enjoyed by the emperor. Chinese emperors were absolute rulers who had total authority over their lands; they were regarded as the mediators between heaven and earth, and as such their pronouncements were unchallengeable.

### Gohei

This Shinto symbol represents offerings to the gods. Every Shinto temple contains *gohei*—a metal frame hanging with strips of paper that flutter in the wind. This ritual object is carried by the priest to attract the deity to his temple with the lure of rich offerings. In times of drought the gohei is carried in procession in order to bring rain. It was used in the Japanese myth of Amaterasu to entice the sun-goddess out of her cave.

### Goose

The "Immortal Gander" is a Hindu myth that first appears in the Mahabharata, the spiritual Sanskrit epic of gods and demons, battles, loves, and hates. The goose is at home on water, in the skies, and on the ground, so it is the natural mount of the creator Brahma for his journeys around the world. Thanks to this versatility the goose is a symbol of the two contrasting aspects of the human condition—spirituality and earthbound desires. It is also a symbol of knowledge and intelligence.

### Gourd

The hollowed out and dried fruit of the calabash has been long used by travelers as a water carrier. Prized by the Taoists, double gourds *(hu-lu)* are a lucky symbol that symbolizes the union of yin and yang and heaven and earth. When smoke issues from the gourd it is to ward off evil spirits. The double gourd is an attribute of Li T'ieh-kuai, one of the Eight Immortals of the Taoists.

### Ho-ho bird

This mythical bird is the Japanese equivalent of the phoenix, with the body of a pheasant and the tail feathers of a peacock. It appears at the start of a new era, does good deeds, and then returns to heaven to await the next era. It became a symbol of imperial power and authority, especially for the empress, as it symbolizes honesty, justice, obedience, loyalty, humility, and sincerity. Said to mate for life, the ho-ho bird was often depicted on wedding gifts.

### Magnolia

The beautiful magnolia tree with its large waxy white flowers held upright on the boughs is called *mu-lan* in ancient Chinese; it symbolized gentleness and female beauty. Magnolias belonged only to the emperor, but he would bestow a plant as an exceptional token of royal favor. A magnolia tree was believed to have grown out of the tomb of Confucius.

### Magpie

In Chinese *his ch'iao* or "bird of joy," the magpie features in many folk stories and superstitions. Two magpies together symbolize married happiness. The calling of a magpie foretells the arrival of good news or of a visitor. Three magpies sitting in a tree in the sunshine symbolize the coming fortune of three joys; twelve magpies signify twelve good wishes. A Manchu legend tells how a magpie settled on the founder of the dynasty and succeeded in deceiving the enemies who were chasing him. Since then it has been a sacred bird.

## Mandala

*Mandala* is a Sanskrit word meaning meditation, and the symbol itself represents the universe. It is a circle enclosing a square with four "doors" to the north, east, south, and west. Often an image of the Buddha is placed in the center and he is sometimes accompanied by his four Dhyani-Buddhas, each enclosed within a circle; other times it can be a demon. The mandala is used as the channel for meditation, especially by Tibetan Lamaists but also in India, China, and Indonesia.

## Narcissus

In Chinese *shui-hsien-hua,* narcissus, means water immortal or nymph. It is a symbol of good fortune for the coming year provided it blooms at Chinese New Year, then it will bring good fortune for the next twelve months. It is one of the Eight Taoist Immortals. It is also one of the Chinese Four Nobilities along with plum, cinnamon, and chrysanthemum. In Greek mythology the narcissus symbolizes deadly vanity and self-absorption; the youth Narcissus fell in love with his own reflection and was unable to look away until he eventually faded away to become this beautiful flower.

## Orange

Heavily scented white orange blossom is a symbol of purity and virginity and is traditionally carried in a bride's bouquet. In the Far East the fruit itself is a traditional gift at Chinese and Japanese New Year celebrations. In China the presentation of oranges on the second day of New Year symbolizes the hope for good luck during the next twelve months, and when given to a married woman the hope that she will soon have children.

### Origins of the universe

This ancient Tibetan symbol is used to refer to the origins of the universe. It shows the seed from which the universe grew as it spun in a clockwise direction into a spiral of energy. Briefly, in the primal chaos a breeze moved and grew ever stronger. Eventually it formed a double thunderbolt, Dorje Gyatram, from which clouds grew and huge raindrops fell, creating the cosmic ocean, Chi Gyatso. Gradually the wind churned the ocean until it solidified to form the earth in the shape of a great mountain, Rirab Lhumpo. Winds swirled around it and salty rain fell and formed the oceans. So the universe was made with Rirab Lhumpo, the home of the gods, in the center.

### Paintbrush

The Chinese use a brush-pen with which to write and revere it as one of the Four Treasures of the scholar. As the tool of calligraphy and painting the brush symbolizes learning and wisdom. A brush is the attribute of K'uei Hsing, the demonic god of literature, and when a scholar is particularly gifted he is called "a brush of five colors" in allusion to the different types of animal hair that make a good brush.

### Peach

This small fruit tree possesses great significance for the Chinese. Called *t'ao,* the peach is a symbol of spring—the time of year it flowers—of eternal renewal and longevity. As a gift for newlyweds, a peach symbolizes happiness; the written character means both peach and marriage. But peach blossom alludes to an early death, while a fallen blossom symbolizes a prostitute. According to Taoist legend Hsi Wang Mu, the Queen Mother of the West, guards the peaches of immortality that grow in her palace gardens. Peach wood is believed to repel evil spirits, so it is used for carving the figures that guard doorways.

## Peony

This beautiful but short-lived flower is very popular in both China *(mu-tan)* and Japan *(botan-kwa)* and is frequently depicted on paintings, ceramics, and costumes. Although it is considered a yang plant, it symbolizes feminine beauty, love, and the female virtues in general. For Chinese the tree peony is one of the Four Seasons (with the lotus, plum, and chrysanthemum) and a symbol of spring. For Japanese it is a symbol of imperial power and huge wealth as well as signifying spring and feminine virtues.

## Pine tree

In Japanese culture this is one of the Three Friends of Winter — along with bamboo and plum blossom — and is called *matsu-no-ke.* The Japanese use pine branches around gates at New Year to attract good fortune because pine trees are believed to be the temporary homes of the gods while they visit earth. In China the pine symbolizes winter and long life as well as hope and good fortune. At one time pines were planted on graves to ward off evil spirits.

## Plum

The plum tree *(li)* is of great significance to Chinese culture. Belonging to the Four Seasons, the late-winter-blooming wild plum is the symbol of winter. It is also one of the Three Friends of Winter (the other two being bamboo and pine) that symbolize good luck and long life. Plum trees are considered to be especially tough plants, so they symbolize steadfastness. Also, the delicate white plum blossom symbolizes the integrity of Confucian scholars, and many poets, writers, and painters celebrate the delicate blossom.

### Rhinoceros

A symbol of good omen to early Taoists, who believed that its horn contained magical properties, in particular a powerful aphrodisiac. Unfortunately for the poor rhino, this has led to widescale slaughter by poachers. It was also believed that if the horn were used as a drinking vessel it would disintegrate or sweat if the drink were poisoned. For the Chinese the rhino is one of the Eight Treasures and a pair of crossed horns symbolize joy.

### Shou

This Chinese character symbolizes long life or immortality and comes from Taoist philosophy. It is a frequently depicted symbol found on a variety of objects such as paintings, textiles, and ceramics. Many variants of the symbol are known but they all mean the same thing. The symbol is often placed alongside other Chinese symbols of longevity such as the pine tree, the tortoise, or the crane, and placed on wedding gifts to bestow the blessing of a long and happy life together.

### Sword

Swords are important symbols of power and authority and also of justice and strength. When an enemy yields his sword he symbolically concedes the fight, and in the case of a king, his country. A long, sharp blade is the universal weapon, and it features in many cultures. For Taoists a sword symbolizes victory over the powers of darkness; for Hindu deities it shows their almighty power and is often shown flaming. More subtly, for Buddhists the sword cuts through ignorance and doubt and so symbolizes wisdom and insight. In Christianity many saints and apostles carry a sword to show the might of the word of Christ.

## Treasure vase

A lidded jar is one of the Eight Lucky Emblems (or Auspicious Symbols) of Buddhism and is known as "the vase of inexhaustible treasures." Modeled on a traditional Indian clay pot, it is often very ornate, with symbolic flames emerging from the top and lotus petal designs on the side. However much is removed from it the vase remains full. It symbolizes a long and healthy life of freedom, wealth, and ease. In ancient Tibetan custom such vases (*norbum*) were filled with precious things and left on altars or buried near important places to increase spiritual and material wealth and to protect from bad spirits.

## Trigram

This symbol, called *pa kua,* was worn as an amulet for good fortune and embellished the dress of important military personnel and religious leaders. There are eight ancient Chinese divinatory trigrams, each made up of a different combination of three lines. An unbroken line is yang and a broken line yin. Legend says that they were revealed to the emperor Fu Hsi (c. 2852 B.C.) while he was meditating on the pattern of a tortoise shell. When the trigram is used for divination the lines are presented in a circle with the yin and yang motif in the center.

## Two seeds of resistance

A Japanese samurai heraldic sign known as *mon* symbolizes the two seeds of the universe rotating counter-clockwise. Samurai were essentially aristocratic mounted archers who formed an elite fighting class. They followed a strict ethical system called the Code of Bushido, which consisted of ideals drawn from a mixture of the philosophies of Buddha, Confucius, Chu-Tsu, and the ancient gods of the Shinto faith. The ethics had eight points: Jin, Gi, Chu, Ko, Rei, Chi, Shin, and Tei, and dealt with respect and truth.

### Wheel of life

Also called the wheel of teaching or the wheel of doctrine, the Dharma-cakra, it symbolizes the way Buddhist teaching will roll over and crush falsehood. Also, the eight spokes symbolize the eight paths of Buddhism: to possess the right knowledge, the right state of mind, the right action, the right speech, the right way of living, the right way of trying, the right vigilance, and the right meditation. Buddha took the title Cakravartin, meaning "he who turns the wheel"— that is, he who rules the universe. Before Buddha assumed a recognizable physical form this wheel was his symbol; it later came to represent Buddhist teaching.

### Wood

For the Chinese wood is symbolic of the east and the season of spring. The Chinese believed that wood came from water but could be destroyed by metal; when burned it produces fire and can destroy earth; it is one of the Five Elements and symbolizes flexibility.

### Yin and yang

The yin and yang symbol is well known the world over, it is sometimes also referred to as the Tai-Chi symbol. The top part represents the sun (yang) and the lower part the moon (yin). Originally it was Chinese, from the I-Ching, which was the foundation of Chinese philosophy. This was based on the concept that we should emulate the natural phenomena of our universe in order to find peace with the world and ourselves.

# Early Culture Symbols

Early cultures across the world developed different means of communicating and recording events. Today we know this by the marks left as glyphs or drawings, generally on stone and rocks. The Mayan glyphs carved many thousands of years ago are so complex that they are still confounding the archaeologists who unearth them.

Norse runes are a range of pictographs used by the peoples of northern Europe. Their origins can be found in Bronze Age Scandinavian rock carvings, although it is thought that they were first used around the first and second centuries B.C. The similarities between the runes and the modern alphabet are not coincidental, but how this came about is not known.

One of the early titles given to the runic system was "Futhark"—this name was created by putting the first six symbols together. Originally consisting of twenty-four letters, it was used by the tribes of what

is now Sweden, Norway, Denmark, and northern Germany. Also known as the Elder, or Germanic, Futhark, it was in use until the eighth century A.D. A later system, the Anglo-Saxon "Futhorc," is thought to have appeared in the fifth century A.D.; essentially similar, it had additional symbols and changed existing ones. The "Younger Futhark" was used by tribes of Denmark, Sweden, and Norway. The Vikings spread it to Iceland and Greenland, and may have even taken it on their early voyages to America.

The runes were still used well into the seventeenth century, but in 1639 the Christian church declared them to be associated with the devil and banned them from use. They were largely disused until the rise of fascism in the 1930s, when they were revived as symbols in Nazi "racial purity" propaganda. This made them unpopular until their use was revived in the latter part of the twentieth century.

### F—Fehu

The Fehu rune is the first symbol in the Futhark alphabet and is known as the "Rune of Cattle" or the "Rune of Right Nourishment"; it represents many things, including prosperity, wealth, self-esteem, and karma. The Fehu rune is also associated with the Norse myths of Freyr and Sigurd, and symbolizes the concept of simple domestic pleasures, such as hard work and good living. In the spiritual sense, it is associated with the need to return home after traveling.

### U—Uruz

The Uruz symbol is known as the "Rune of the Aurochs" or the "Rune of Endurance"; it represents a variety of things, such as strength, power, energy, fertility, and the unconscious mind. Aurochs were a primitive species of upland ox, known for their strength and endurance in adverse conditions. When referred to for magical purposes, Uruz is used for strengthening the power of the mind, and particularly for hunting. The Uruz rune is associated with the Norse myths of Odin.

### TH—Thurisaz

Thurisaz is known as the "Rune of the Giant" or the "Rune of Blind Force"; it represents hardship, discipline, knowledge, and bad times. It is referred to in magic as the symbol of meditation and self-discipline, and is considered to be representative of obstacles we have to learn to deal with and overcome in our lives. The Thurisaz rune is associated with the Norse myths of the Frost Giants and Loki.

### A—Ansuz

The Ansuz symbol is known as the "Rune of Odin" or the "Rune of Omens"; it represents figures of authority as well as equilibrium, balance, and justice. Odin was the Norse god of war but also the god of wisdom. He was revered for his leadership skills, as well as for those of a shaman. This rune often means a signal or message, and in magic it may indicate success, wise decisions, or strong leadership.

### R—Raido

The Raido symbol is known as the "Rune of the Wagon" or the "Rune of Right Action"; it represents planning before long journeys, be they physical or spiritual. It may be taken to mean several things, including pilgrimages, quests, or the following of destiny, and indicates that persistence and strategy are important if success is to be achieved. The Raido rune is used in magic as protection for travelers, and is associated with the Norse myth of Sigurd's journey.

### K—Kenaz

The Kenaz symbol is known as the "Rune of the Torch" or the "Rune of Ingenuity"; it represents wisdom, creativity, inspiration, and enlightenment. The meaning of this symbol lives on today in the Scottish word *ken,* which means "to know." The Kenaz rune is used in magic to help in learning and for creative inspiration, as well as for fertility and allaying fears and anxieties. It is associated with the Norse myths of the Dwarves.

### G — Gebo

The Gebo symbol is known as the "Rune of Partnership" or the "Rune of the Ritual of Commitment." It represents a connection between people or an exchange of gifts; it may also mean trust, love, marriage, partnership, or good fortune. It can also symbolize important oaths or bonds. It is used in magic to strengthen relationships, improve fertility, or bring luck. The Gebo rune is associated with the Norse myths of Sigurd and Brunhild.

### W — Wunjo

The Wunjo symbol is known as the "Rune of Joy" or the "Rune of Harmonious Merging"; it represents joy and fulfillment, and indicates success in some endeavor, rewards, or the recognition of the achievement of goals. It also symbolizes stability, but in the sense of a resting point on a long journey. It is used in magic to help with motivation or to help in the completion of difficult tasks. The Wunjo rune is associated with the Norse myths of Baldr and Asgard.

### H — Hagalaz

The Hagalaz symbol is known as the "Rune of Disruption"; it represents great loss, ordeal, destruction, drastic change, or disaster. It is used in magic to help break destructive patterns or remove unwanted influences, and is associated with the Norse myths of Ragnarok, Loki, and the Frost Giants. The significance in this symbol is that it indicates that the old must die or be destroyed to make way for the new.

### N—Nauthiz

The Nauthiz symbol is known as the "Rune of Necessity" or the "Rune of the Forging of Character"; it represents poverty, hardship, responsibility, obstacles, or frustration. In magic it indicates a need of some description, and is used to help identify priorities or to help create a desire to instigate change. It is associated with the Norse myths of Freyr and Gurd, and also the Otter's Gold. This rune may also show that whatever one may have, it is not enough.

### I—Isa

The Isa symbol is known as the "Rune of Ice" or the "Rune of Waiting"; it represents inactivity, stagnation, unfulfilled potential, or patience. Probably derived from the need to wait for long Norse winters to end, it symbolizes both a threat to livelihood and the creation of life when spring returns. The Isa rune is used in magic to prevent untoward things from happening. It is associated with the Norse myths of Nifelheim.

### J—Jera

The Jera symbol is known as the "Rune of the Harvest" or the "Rune of Fruition"; it represents change, reward, productivity, and the passing of cycles such as the seasons. It is used in magic to help bring about change or to promote fertility and growth. The Jera rune is associated with the Norse myths of Thor and Freyr, and symbolizes the need to enjoy life by reaping pleasures while you can.

### EI—Eihwaz

The Eihwaz symbol is known as the "Rune of Defense" or the "Rune of Testing"; it represents change, facing up to fears, turning points, or death. It symbolizes the evergreen yew tree, and as such indicates long life, especially in the dead of winter, and is used in magic to help bring about important changes. The Eihwaz rune is particularly associated with rites of passage, and this is reflected in the Norse myths of Hel and Yggdrasil.

### P—Pertho

The Pertho symbol is known as the "Rune of Secrets" or the "Rune of the Web of Fate"; it represents rebirth after death, and the maternal attributes of fertility, sexuality, and new beginnings, as well as prophecy, mystery, magic, and divination. It is used in magic to promote fertility, ease childbirth, enhance psychic powers, and help in divining portents. The Pertho rune is associated with the Norse myths of Freya and Angrbode.

### A/Z—Algiz

The Algiz symbol is known as the "Rune of Protection" or the "Rune of Watchfulness"; it represents protection, assistance, defense, warning, and support in adversity. It may also indicate a spiritual helper, guide, or mentor. It is used in magic to give protection and to make hunting more successful, and is associated with the Norse myths of Heimdall (a protector and guardian who watches the gates between worlds) and Gjallerhorn.

### S—Sowilo

The Sowilo symbol is known as the "Rune of Sunlight" or the "Rune of Wholeness"; it represents motion, life, and fertility, as well as many other positive things, including success, energy, power, activity, and health. It is used in magic to promote all such positive things, as well as physical and emotional strength, and healing after illness or injury. The Sowilo rune is associated with the Norse myths of Sunna.

### T—Teiwaz

The Teiwaz symbol is known as the "Rune of Justice" or the "Rune of the Warrior"; it represents the attributes revered by Norsemen of heroism, duty, discipline, responsibility, self-sacrifice, conflict, and strength. Likewise, it is used in magic for providing protection, bringing victory, increasing physical and emotional strength, and healing wounds. The theme of the responsibility of the warrior continues in Norse myths, where this symbol is associated with Odin's ordeals.

### B—Berkana

The Berkana symbol is known as the "Rune of the Goddess" or the "Rune of Transition"; it represents the birch tree, itself a symbol of fertility. It also indicates health, new beginnings, growth, conception, or a time of plenty. The medicinal properties of the birch tree mean that it is used in magic as a symbol of healing infections, for promoting fertility, or for instigating changes. Birch trees grow very rapidly, so this also made it a natural symbol for growth.

### E—Ehwaz

The Ehwaz symbol is known as the "Rune of the Horse" or the "Rune of Effective Partnership"; it represents many of the positive attributes of the horse—transportation, motion, assistance, power, and will—but also that of recklessness. The Ehwaz rune is used in magic to increase one's powers to help communications and transportation, and to send spells. It is associated with the Norse myths of Sleipnir and Freya's feathered cloak.

### M—Mannaz

The Mannaz symbol is known as the "Rune of Humanity" or the "Rune of Individuality"; it represents mankind in all its many forms: the identities of self, family, and community, as well as those of relationships and social situations. The Mannaz rune is used in magic to indicate a person or group of people, and also to help build social bonds. It is associated with the Norse myths of the Midgard serpent.

### L—Laguz

The Laguz symbol is known as the "Rune of the Sea" or the "Rune of Release"; it represents emotions, unresolved fears, and the unconscious mind. Since it represents water, and in particular the sea, it symbolizes both the calm and the unpredictable. It is used in magic to enhance psychic abilities, to help deal with fears, to calm the mind, and to discover hidden secrets. The Laguz rune's associations with the sea make it closely tied into the Norse myths of the Midgard serpent.

### NG—Ingwuz

The Ingwuz symbol is known as the "Rune of Fertility" or the "Rune of Rebirth"; it represents honest hard work, productivity, times of plenty, balance, and farming. Ing was the Norse God of agriculture and fertility, and so this connection is carried through in magic where the rune is used to improve fertility and yields from the land, and to assist general health. Ingwuz is associated with the Norse myths of Thor and Freyr—a Danish name for Ing.

### D—Dagaz

The Dagaz symbol is known as the "Rune of Dawn" or the "Rune of Breakthrough"; it represents satisfaction, happiness, success, and a meaningful life. The symbolism of the sun returning to stave off the dark of night and bring the light of another day was important to the peoples of northern Europe. This rune was used in magic to help create a positive outcome to an important situation.

### O—Othala

The Othala symbol is known as the "Rune of Retreat" or the "Rune of Regrouping"; it represents long-term material associations and possessions, such as property and land, as well as less tangible things like a sense of belonging and the concept of "home." It is used in magic to help in the acquisition of property, to assist in the completion of projects, and to strengthen bonds within families and organizations.

### Ancient sun sign

This ancient emblem is symbolic of the sun, which in turn is symbolic of male power in many cultures. The three rays show the sun's radiance, with the cross strokes symbolizing the vault of the heavens. For the ancient Indian Vedic culture the sun belonged to the god Surya, a solar god who rode across the sky in a fiery chariot. He was one of three elements comprising air (Vayu), fire (Agni), and sun (Surya).

### Elf cross

The elf cross, also called the ella cross, is an ancient symbol from Sweden. Crosses like this were carved or painted on and around houses to protect the home and its inhabitants from evil, in particular trolls. In Scandinavian mythology elves were somewhat malign spirits who lived and hunted in the vast forests; they loved nature but could be vindictive and dangerous to cross.

### Turtle

In Native American culture the turtle symbolizes the earth and the earth mother, and the turtle is credited with saving mankind from exile after a mighty flood. The ancient Chinese believed that the eight Taoist immortals lived on the Islands of the Blessed, which floated on the backs of huge turtles. In Polynesian cultures the turtle symbolizes the immense powers belonging to the gods of the oceans. Australian Aborigines also see the turtle as symbolic of water and safety at sea.

## Pop

This is the Maya glyph for the first month of the year, Pop. The Mayans used a complex system of date keeping, much of which predated their civilization. They counted time in Great Cycles, which correspond roughly with Western time periods of millennia, centuries, etc. They calculated their 260-day count (the Tzolk'n almanac) to make the solar 365-day year. It took approximately fifty-two years—the long count—before the same date recurred. According to current calculations the last Great Cycle began on August 13, 3114 B.C. and will end on December 23, A.D. 2012.

## K'ayab

This is the Maya glyph for the seventeenth month, K'ayab. Mayans sowed and harvested their crops according to the calendar, and the date was vitally important for state ceremonies and celebrations as well as for religious observations. Furthermore, the Mayans used their calendar for fortune-telling and forecasting. Mayan civilization covered the Yucatán peninsula of Mexico and the area that is now Guatemala. But much about the Maya is still a mystery, with only the remnants of a few surviving books along with their myths and legends to give any real idea of their lives.

## Wayeb

Wayeb is the only Mayan month that lasts for five days. The Yucatec Mayan had a solar calendar of nineteen named months in their year (haab): Pop, Uo, Sip, Sotz, Tzec, Xul, Yaxk'in, Mol, Ch'en, Yax, Sac, Keh, Mak, K'ank'in, Muwan, Pax, K'ayab, Kumk'u, and Wayeb. Each of these lasts twenty days with the exception of the last, which was dreaded by Mayans, as it was believed to be an unlucky time.

**Early Culture Symbols**

# Astrology, Mysticism, and Myth

### Astrological

The signs of the zodiac are a series of symbols that represent an imaginary belt in the heavens. Divided into twelve constellations, each is associated with a particular object. A person's zodiac or star sign is determined by the position of the sun when they are born. A horoscope is a chart that depicts the position of the planets as seen from Earth when the person was born. The interpretation of horoscopes is an art that is several thousand years old.

### Chinese Astrological

The Chinese zodiac is based on a twelve-year cycle with the year changing on the first new moon of the following year. Each year is represented by an animal that is believed to impose certain characteristics on the type of year it will be and also on the people born within that period. Each animal also rules two hours of every day. The animal names are a traditional folk method for naming and remembering the years.

### Mystical

Mystical symbols are often referred to as "pagan"—a term often considered synonymous with black magic, but deriving from the Latin *paganus,* meaning a country dweller or villager. In modern times, "paganism" is used to refer to a wide range of magic-embracing religions, many of which use a system to represent the objects, entities, seasons, emotions, and features of mystical life; some are intuitive, others are not. They all have specific meanings, many of which are important to parts of mystical and magical ceremonies.

### Mythical

Some of the more common mythical symbols are derived from Greek and Roman legends. For our ancestors, the gods and goddesses dominated a particular facet of life—such as health, fertility, good fortune, or victory in battle—and would be appealed to when their individual talents were needed. Many gods appear in different aspects, determined by additional symbols.

## Aries

Aries is the sign of the ram, and its glyph is thought to represent the curve of the ram's horns. Aries begins at the spring equinox—which is also the start of the zodiac year—when the sun enters the house of Aries. The astrological period of Aries lies between March 21 and April 20. Rams were associated in ancient times with the season of spring and thus with fertility, new beginnings, and creative energy. In Christianity St. Peter is linked with the ram, as was Minerva in ancient Greece, and the Egyptian gods Amun, Osiris, and Khnum.

## Taurus

Taurus is the sign of the bull, and its symbol represents a bull's head with upright horns. The astrological period of Taurus lies between April 21 and May 20. The bull was historically associated with strength and power, and the bull god Apis was worshiped for thousands of years in ancient Egypt. In Greek mythology, Zeus changed himself into a white bull with golden horns in an attempt to seduce the beautiful Europa.

## Gemini

Gemini is the sign of the twins, and this is reflected in the symbol, which shows twin characters. The astrological period of Gemini lies between May 21 and June 21. The name Gemini is a translation of the Greek word *didymoi,* meaning twins. Although no one knows who the twins originally were, they are generally thought to be the Greek twins Castor and Pollux, who reputedly had different fathers, one of whom was mortal and the other the god Zeus.

**Astrology, Mysticism, and Myth**

### Cancer

Cancer is the sign of the crab. The astrological period of Cancer lies between June 22 and July 22. "Cancer" is derived from Greek mythology, where it was referred to as Karkinos, and was one of Hera's pet animals. Hercules killed Hera's crab as the second of his twelve great labors. The astronomical constellations were probably first discovered by the Babylonians, who called Cancer "Nangar."

### Leo

Leo is the sign of the lion. The astrological period of Leo lies between July 23 and August 22. The name Leo means lion, and the symbol represents the lion's mane, although it can also symbolize the warmth of the sun. In ancient times the lion was associated with leadership, and its characteristics were thought to be directly linked to the gods; in more modern times the lion has been used to symbolize guardianship and protection. The Babylonians called Leo "U-ra."

### Virgo

Virgo is the sign of the Virgin. The astrological period of Virgo lies between August 23 and September 22. The ancient Egyptians called this sign "the maiden," and the Babylonians called it "Absin"; it has been linked in Christianity with Dina, the only daughter of Jacob. The constellation of Virgo is at the center of the closest large cluster of galaxies, and is about 70 million light years from Earth.

## Libra

Libra is the sign of the scales or the balance. The astrological period of Libra lies between September 23 and October 22. The Roman goddess of justice, Astraea, was said to have carried scales in which she weighed the good deeds and sins of mortal people. She was so disillusioned by the wickedness of humanity that she left earth to join the heavens. The Romans found she had left her scales behind, and terrified of her power, they placed them in the constellation Libra, which the Babylonians called "Zihanitum."

## Scorpio

Scorpio is the sign of the scorpion. The astrological period of Scorpio lies between October 23 and November 21. In Greek mythology, Scorpio was the mortal enemy of the hunter Orion, and was ordered by the gods to spring a trap and poison Orion with his sharp sting. This he did, and even Aesculapius, the god of healing, could not revive him from the fatal toxin. The Babylonians called Scorpio "Gir-tab."

## Sagittarius

Sagittarius is the sign of the archer. The astrological period of Sagittarius lies between November 22 and December 21. The origin of the story of the archer lies in Greek mythology: when Zeus's father Cronus was trying to seduce Philyra, he hid from his jealous wife in the form of a stallion. A child was born that was half man, half horse—a centaur. He was granted immortality by Zeus in the form of the constellation Sagittarius, which the Babylonians called "Pah."

### Capricorn

Capricorn is the sign of the goat. The astrological period of Capricorn lies between December 22 and January 19. The constellation of Capricornus is also known as the "sea goat," and may be represented as an animal with the body of a goat and the tail of a fish—this was sometimes interpreted to be the god Pan changing himself into a sea creature. The sea goat may also be shown as a dolphin. The Babylonians called Capricorn "Suhur."

### Aquarius

Aquarius is the sign of the water bearer or carrier. The astrological period of Aquarius lies between January 20 and February 18. Water is symbolic of the unconscious, and since pre-Babylonian times, the sign of Aquarius has always been associated with a man or boy carrying an urn, bucket, or jar of water. The Babylonians called the sign "Gu" or "Gula." In Greek mythology the water bearer was called "Ganymedes," which means "rejoicing in virility."

### Pisces

Pisces is the sign of the fishes. The astrological period of Pisces lies between February 19 and March 20. The constellation of Pisces was one of the first to be recognized in ancient times. In mythology it represented the goddess Venus and her son Cupid, who changed themselves into fish and jumped into the River Nile to escape the monster Typhon. The Babylonians called Pisces "Nunu," which means fish; this was also symbolic to early Christians, to whom it represented the miracle of the loaves and fishes.

### Rat

The rat is the first animal in the Chinese twelve-year cycle and so ranks first in precedence. Its season is decreed to be winter, its direction due north, and its fixed element water. The rat rules the hours of 11 P.M. to 1 A.M. and is a yang (positive) sign. For Chinese, the rat is a creature symbolizing wealth and abundance accrued by its hoarding character. The rat's habit of nibbling at everything and anything causes it to be seen as a symbol for the acquisition of knowledge.

### Ox

The second animal in the Chinese zodiac. Its season is midwinter, its direction is north-northeast, and its fixed element water. The ox is supposed to rule the hours of 1 A.M. to 3 A.M. and is a yin (negative) sign. In China the ox is associated with the rebirth of the land in spring and with fertility, probably because in ancient times oxen were used to break the soil in ceremonial spring plowing. They are gentle, domesticated animals and are often portrayed as being ridden by Taoist deities, in particular the sage Laozi. For Buddhists the ox is a sacred animal, and Chinese Buddhists in particular revere the white ox, which symbolizes wise thought.

### Tiger

The third sign of the Chinese zodiac, the tiger symbolizes courage, power, passion, and aggression. The tiger's season is late winter, its direction lies east-northeast, and its fixed element is wood. The tiger is supposed to rule the hours of 3 A.M. to 5 A.M. and is a yang sign. Tigers were often used on ancient Chinese graves because they were believed to protect the dead against evil spirits. A white tiger represented the West in the ancient system of the four cardinal directions. The tiger is a popular image in many cultures and always symbolizes bravery.

# 貓 龍 蛇

### Hare

The hare or rabbit is the fourth sign of the Chinese zodiac. The hare symbolizes long life and is said to collect his essence from the moon. Its season is early spring, its fixed element wood, and its direction due east. The rabbit rules the hours of 5 A.M. until 7 A.M. and is a yin animal. Inextricably linked with the moon in many cultures, it is often associated with moon goddesses as well as with fecundity due to its prolific rate of procreation.

### Dragon

The fifth sign of the Chinese zodiac, symbolic of good fortune and energy. Its season is midspring, its direction east-southeast, and its fixed element wood. It rules the hours 7 A.M. to 9 A.M. and is a yang sign. In China dragons are called "lung" and are believed to be benevolent divinities and rain bringers— the lord of the waters, including marshes, lakes, rivers, seas, and clouds. Chinese dragons have the head of a camel with the eyes of a demon, plus the horns of a stag, ears of a bull, long whiskers of a cat, the neck of a snake, the scales of a fish, and the pads of a tiger, with the claws of an eagle—they are often shown flying even though they don't have wings.

### Snake

The snake is the sixth sign of the Chinese zodiac and represents cleverness and treachery. Its season is late spring, its direction south-southeast, and its fixed element fire. The snake is supposed to rule the hours of 9 A.M. until 11 A.M. and is a yin sign. The Chinese also equate snakes with sexual energy and sensuality. In China the snake is one of the "Five Poisons" (along with the toad, centipede, scorpion, and spider), which are believed to ward off evil and illness but also are, of course, lethally poisonous. Buddhists despise snakes because, along with cats, they did not weep when Buddha died.

### Horse

The seventh animal in the Chinese zodiac, the horse symbolizes good luck. Its season is decreed to be summer, its direction due south, and its fixed element fire. The horse is supposed to rule the hours of 11 A.M. to 1 P.M. and it is a yang sign. Followers of Buddha revere horses, especially white horses that are symbolical of purity and faithfulness. The horse is one of the Seven Treasures of Buddha, symbolic of indestructibility.

### Goat

Also sometimes shown as a sheep, this is the eighth-ranked animal of the Chinese zodiac. Its season is midsummer, its direction south-southwest, and its fixed element fire. The goat is supposed to rule the hours of 1 P.M. to 3 P.M. and is a yin sign. The Chinese word for goat is pronounced the same as the words for "male" and "sun," so it is symbolic of masculinity and sunshine but also of goodness and peaceful times. The Chinese goat spirit is Yang Chin (who is also a Mongolian god); he has a white face with a long beard, horns, and wears a special headdress.

### Monkey

The ninth-ranked animal of the Chinese zodiac, its season is late summer, its direction west-southwest, and its fixed element metal. The monkey rules the hours of 3 P.M. to 5 P.M. and is a yang sign. Monkeys are often depicted as mischief makers, and in Chinese legends are frequently the instigators of trouble. The most popular Chinese monkey is Sun Wukung, the monkey king of legend who appears in the story "Monkey." He became immortal by erasing his name from the list of the dead and then eating the peaches of immortality.

# 鶏 犬 猪

## Rooster

The rooster, or sometimes chicken, is the tenth animal sign of the Chinese zodiac. Its season is decreed to be early fall, its direction due west, and its fixed element metal. The rooster is supposed to rule the hours of 5 P.M. to 7 P.M. and is a yin sign. Chinese like to place a white rooster on a loved one's coffin to keep away ghosts.

## Dog

The dog is the eleventh sign of the Chinese zodiac. Its season is midfall, its direction west-northwest, and its fixed element metal. The dog is supposed to rule the hours of 7 P.M. to 9 P.M. and is a yang sign. T'ien-kou is the Celestial Dog who lives in the Pole Star and chases wicked spirits on the orders of his master, Erh Lang. Although he is reputed to eat babies, by default he guards their cradles and catches the evil spirits that are attracted to helpless newborns.

## Boar

Also known as the pig, this is the twelfth and last sign of the twelve-year Chinese zodiac. Its season is decreed to be late fall, its direction north-northwest, and its fixed element water. The boar is supposed to rule the hours of 9 P.M. until 11 P.M. and is a yin sign. In the Chinese legends about the journeys and adventures of Monkey, one of his companions is the pig spirit Chu Pa Chieh, known as Pigsy.

### Spring

The onset of spring has been a powerful sign in human cultures for tens of thousands of years: it has direct symbolic associations with fertility and is often celebrated with carnivals or festivals. The great significance of spring's arrival was due to the concept that it is time of resurrection for the plants and animals that had "died" during winter. Today the Christian festival of Easter is closely associated with spring, but it was originally a pagan celebration named after the Anglo Saxon maiden goddess Eostre, who was associated with fertility.

### Summer

Summer has special significance in mystical cultures—it is a season of activity and energy, beginning with the month of June. The summer solstice takes place over June 21st to the 23rd, with Midsummer's Eve heralding the longest day of the year. The sun is at its highest and most powerful at this time, a fact that has held significance from early human cultures to the present day. From Midsummer's Day onward, the sun starts waning, and continues to do so until the winter solstice.

### Fall

The fall is considered in mystical terms to be a time of balance between the light of summer and the dark of winter. It is a time of thanksgiving, when celebrations mark the completion of the harvest and offerings are made to show appreciation for the resulting plenty. The fall equinox is between September 21st and 23rd, and marks the time when preparations for winter begin, both for humans and wildlife.

Astrology, Mysticism, and Myth

### Winter

In mystical terms, winter is seen as a time of death: many plants and animals die, and it is a season of hardship for all. The winter solstice takes place between December 21st and 23rd; it marks the longest night of the year, when darkness rules and the new sun is finally born. The time was originally marked by pagan celebrations that are now known as Christmas, and by the lighting of candles and Yule Logs or bonfires to symbolize giving life and power to the sun.

### Bane/deadly

This symbol represents the circle of life held within the cross of death. It therefore symbolizes that which can be harmful, destructive, or evil to life. The magical act of banishment is used to end an unwanted process, remove the presence of an unwanted being or spirit, or exorcise entities from a person or place. Banishment is also the act of formally dismantling a magic circle when it is finished with after a ritual or ceremony has been completed.

### Blessings

Blessings can take many forms in mystical or magical terms—for instance, people can be blessed when they get married, when a child is born, or when a warrior is going to battle. Physical places may also be blessed, such as land upon which crops are to be grown, or magical sites such as streams or springs from which clean water is sought. The "Blessed-Be" is a simple ritual blessing performed by pagans and other cultures as a form of greeting or farewell. It is derived from an ancient rite called the "Five-fold Kiss."

### Cho Ku Rei

This symbol is used in Reiki—an alternative medicine and natural healing technique using the hands of the healer to transfer life force, energy, and health into the patient. Cho Ku Rei is also known as the power symbol. It is pronounced "cho-koo-ray," and is used as an all-purpose symbol for healing or for charging food, herbs, medicines, or other items with Reiki. It may also be used to help remove negative energies from inanimate objects such as houses, shops, factories, and cars. This symbol is also used for general protective purposes.

### Earth

The earth is worshiped by mystics in many ways—for instance, as a religion, in which the worshiper is in harmony with the earth and all life. A different interpretation is that the earth is a power or force that is represented as an energy within natural objects such as stones, herbs, flames, wind, streams, and other natural objects. "Earth magic" is a practical form of mysticism in which energy is drawn from the "Mother Earth," and the vibrations of inanimate objects are controlled for use in rituals.

### Fertility

Fertility has been at the very center of human ritual and religion for tens of thousands of years. The symbol derives from the circle of life, combined with the ancient sign of the egg. The small oval held within a larger one represents the cycle of life and rebirth. The very existence of families and tribes depended on the birth of new generations, both of the people themselves and the animals they lived off of. The fertility of the land was a critical part of this; both the successful harvesting of crops and the hunting of animals were inextricably linked to it.

### Friendship

The magical symbol for friendship is as ancient as human culture itself: two hearts side by side represent the togetherness of two souls. In magic the sign could be used for many reasons, but it was especially important for bestowing good fortune on a relationship or on partners who were separated for extended periods of time due to travel, war, or trade. The friendship sign could also be invoked to help influence the course of romance.

### God

In mysticism, god is paired with goddess, and together they are seen as cocreators of the universe. There are many variations on the theme: some see god as the "Horned Father—Lord of the Forest," whereas others see him as the "Lord of Death and Resurrection." God is associated with the sun, sky, deserts, forests, agriculture, and wild animals. Deities are sometimes also called gods and are seen as immortal beings who may be invoked for "magick."

### Goddess

As with god, there are many different interpretations of the "Goddess" or "Universal Mother"; she is considered to be the supreme female aspect, and is the consort of the "Horned Father." She is also known as the "Powerful Lady Mother," and is the ultimate source of fertility, love, compassion, healing, wisdom, and power, and may be associated with birth and death, as well as the earth, moon, and oceans.

### Healing and health

The magical symbol for healing and health is composed of three ovals of different sizes (with the largest at the top) over a line. The straight line represents the lifeline, and the ovals denote the circles of life — their increasing sizes indicate growth from childhood to adulthood. Overall, the symbol denotes a long, unbroken life of good health. The symbol would be used by magicians in incantations and rituals to invoke help from the spirits in ensuring good health and longevity.

### Hon Sha Ze Sho Nen

The Reiki symbol Hon Sha Ze Sho Nen is also known as the distance symbol. It is pronounced "hone-shaw-zay-show-nen," and represents the method of sending Reiki to anyone (or anything). It is sometimes even used to send healing powers to cure past traumas or to help in the future. It can be interpreted to mean "no past, no present, no future," since some Eastern philosophies consider all time to be happening at the same time.

### Love

The symbol for love is probably the most recognizable sign of all. Across many cultures, the heart has been associated with love for thousands of years, although exactly where it first originated is not known. Magicians would use the love symbol in incantations and rituals for all matters that related to affairs of the heart, such as attempts to influence the course of romance, or to maintain the strength of a relationship.

### Magic circle

The magic circle is a ceremonial site where sacred rites and rituals have been performed since ancient pagan times. The circle symbolizes a portal through which the gods can be reached, and is also a place where boundaries of energy can be created to protect sick people from demons, for instance, or to keep out bad spirits. The circle may be marked on the ground or it may be created from things like ropes or cords; it will often have an altar within it, and there may also be some ritual items as well.

### Magical energy

Magic can take many forms—natural, practical, low, and ceremonial are just a few. Magic itself is not inherently good (white) or bad (black), but is determined by the intentions of the practitioner. It is the practice of inducing supernatural events or controlling natural processes, such as the weather. Practical magic, for instance, is performed with the assistance of simple implements to establish harmony with nature and the seasons. Natural magic uses the power of the magician together with the power of the earth to cause a desired change.

### Marriage

Pagan marriages are sometimes referred to as "Handfastings"—a rite of passage where two people wish to be bonded as partners in the eyes of the gods; they can be bonded for life, for a specified period, or for "as long as love shall last." In the latter case, the two partners are freely allowed to separate and go their own ways should their love end. A high priest or high priestess usually performs the ceremony, which generally takes place between the full moon and the new moon.

### Ourobouros

A serpent in the form of a circle with its tail in its mouth is an *ourobouros,* meaning "tail devouring" in Greek. It is a symbol of time, eternity, and the universe. The concept probably originates from an ancient Egyptian male snake deity with many coils who guarded the world by encircling it with his body, symbolizing the boundlessness of the sea. It also symbolized the precosmic primeval state in which all creation and the sun god renewed themselves every night.

### Peace

The magical symbol for peace is represented by three circles arranged in a triangular manner. These symbolize the circles of life; having three together denotes life bringing forth further life, and therefore that peace reigns. The sign could be used in rituals or incantations to help maintain a peaceful situation, or to try to bring about the end of a war.

### Pentacle

The pentacle is a symbol created by drawing a circle around a five-pointed star; the circle represents earth and the star symbolizes the elements within it. The pentacle has been a significant sign in ceremonies and rituals for thousands of years, and is still used to this day to represent feminine energy in spells and incantations. It is seen by many to represent witchcraft, but to others it is known as the "Pentacle of Solomon."

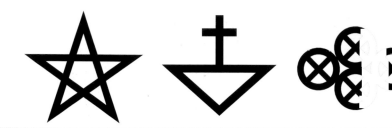

### Pentagram

The pentagram is any drawn symbol based on the pentacle, and is also known as a "witches' star" or a "goblin's cross." The five points usually represent the five elements earth, air, water, fire, and spirit, but the pentagram can also be a symbol of the earth, protection, power, life forces, a witch's belief, or human spiritual aspirations. In some traditions, a pentagram with one point at the top stands for the Goddess, and with two points at the top it represents the Horned God.

### Philosopher's stone

The philosopher's stone was a hypothetical substance that alchemists believed was able to transmute base metals into gold—and therefore into untold riches. Medieval alchemists devoted their lives to the fruitless search, many believing that its basis lay in a mix of pure sulfur and mercury. The philosopher's stone—also called the stone of the wise—was added to the base metal to bring about the transformation. Magically, the philosopher's stone itself would not be affected by the process. (See also "Scientific and Mathematical Symbols.")

### Physical and magical strength

Physical and magical strength are strongly linked; for instance, a magician may focus his or her will and emotions to cause change within themselves to increase their physical strength for some particular purpose. The strength of the "magical voice" also links the two, in that the reading of certain words during rituals or rites must be performed assertively. There must be no room for doubt or insecurity to creep in, whether the words are spoken in whispers, in a speaking voice, or as a song.

### Psychic awareness

Psychic awareness is a condition of mind that mystics strive to attain in order to be able to allow the conscious mind to connect with the psychic mind. It requires that an open mental state be achieved in order for the practitioner to receive psychic messages through the subconscious mind. When two such people simultaneously achieve the correct open psychic state, their minds can link and messages can be exchanged.

### Purification

Purification is an act that dates back thousands of years and may be applied to people, animals, food, or objects. If a person was thought to be possessed by evil spirits, then a purification ceremony would be performed to rid them of the unwanted presence. Acts of ritual purification would take place at springs and wells to ensure that the gods would keep the water clean and free from negative energies. Inanimate objects such as ceremonial crystals would also undergo purification rites before they could be used for magical purposes.

### Rebirth

Rebirth can take many forms, from inanimate things such as the sun or the moon, through to living animals and plants. The sun is considered to be reborn after the winter solstice; likewise, the moon is said to be reborn at the time of the new moon. For thousands of years there have been cultures that have believed that living things are reborn after death. This process is known as reincarnation, and the rebirth may be as another kind of living being, or as the same physical form but with a different level of spiritual achievement.

### Sei He Ki

The Reiki symbol known as Sei He Ki is also known as the mental or emotional symbol. It is pronounced "say-hay-key," and focuses on the energies of the emotional and mental states. It is particularly favored for use in treating past traumas and for protection against evil. It can also be used to turn negative emotions such as fear, depression, or anger into positive ones—this process is considered to be the second stage on the path to enlightenment.

### Spider

In mythology the spider is the weaver of destiny, and deities who foresee the future are very often symbolized by spiders. The spider is an attribute of the Egyptian creator-goddess Neith, who wove the universe, and of the Three Fates, who spun, measured, and then cut the thread of life. In China the spider is one of the Five Poisons but it symbolizes good luck when it spins down on a thread from heaven. In Japan spiders symbolize bad luck.

### Spirituality

Spirituality is an extremely important part of the everyday life of a magician: it is inextricably linked with all the different forms of mystic worship, all of which are directly concerned with the spirituality of nature. Pantheism, for instance, is a belief that all of nature is divine, and animism holds that natural features of the world are invested with divine power. The spiral symbol represents the path leading from outer consciousness to the inner soul.

### Star

The star is a popular symbol in many cultures. For Australian Aborigines the morning star (Venus) is important in the story of life and death and night and day, and symbolizes the moving of the spirit from life into death. For the Sumerians the eight-pointed star symbolized their goddess Inanna. In America the star was used to represent each state of the Union on the flag.

### Sun

Inevitably the sun is an ancient symbol of gods, light, fertility, and life that is significant in many cultures. Many gods—almost always male—are associated with the sun, including Re, Apollo, Mithras, and Helios, all of whom are represented with the sun's rays radiating from their heads. Many sun gods are depicted driving their chariots across the heavens, pulling the sun across the sky. For the ancient Chinese the sun symbolized the male principle (yang) and was a symbol of the emperor.

### To rouse jealousy

The magical sign for rousing jealousy symbolizes the ripples made when a stone is thrown into a pond, representing the waves of cause and effect created by actions or events. These happenings may go on to instill feelings of insecurity or jealousy in others, and may have been deliberately created by bad (black) magicians, and may in turn have to be negated by good (white) magicians. The symbol may therefore be used in incantations or rituals with good or bad intentions.

**Astrology, Mysticism, and Myth**

### Travel

The magical symbol for travel conveys the four points of the compass. Due to the manner in which many zodiacal signs are linked to specific compass directions, it was considered important to perform rituals using the travel symbol to ensure that a traveler would have freedom to move in the desired direction and would meet with good luck. This would be especially significant if a journey was to be made that was not compatible with the current astrological configuration.

### Witch sign

The magical symbol for a witch is often known as the "witch's foot," and may take any one of several forms. The version shown here is composed of three crossed lines within a square; it may also take the form of the symbol that is more commonly thought of as the peace sign. The witch was originally a goddess who led the "wild hunt" on windy, moonlit nights. She was descended from Lilith, the moon goddess of ancient Sumeria, who was depicted with bird's feet because of her affinity to her sacred bird, the owl.

### Yonic

The Yonic symbol is a feminine symbol of protection against all evil, and has been used for hundreds if not thousands of years by witches. The oval shape of the symbol is known as a "vesica" and is often used to create a further symbol called a "triquetra," which is formed by superimposing three yonic vesicas placed at 120 degrees to each other. When it is drawn surrounded by a circle, it becomes what was originally a pagan magical sign of the eternity, representing the triple goddess. Since then it has been incorporated into Christianity to represent the trinity of Father, Son, and Holy Ghost.

100

### Aegricanes

This is the severed head of a ram or goat that the Greeks and Romans used in their temples—especially around the altar—where it symbolized ritual sacrifice. Rams and goats were important animals in classical ritual and were often decorated with garlands of flowers around their necks before being ritually sacrificed to the gods. Greeks and Romans associated goats with licentiousness and fecundity; rams likewise were considered virile and sexually active.

### Boar

The boar was sacred to the Celts, who wore their image on helmets and armor as symbols of strength and courage. For the Celts boars also represented kingship and protection of the land. For the ancient Greeks the boar represented winter and its killing symbolized the triumph of warm spring over cold winter. For Greeks and Romans alike the boar was also Ares/Mars, the god of war, and symbolized strife and destruction. The boar features in one of the labors of Herakles/Hercules and sometimes symbolizes him.

### Bulcranium

This Greco-Roman symbol shows the skull of a ram, bull, ox, or goat, and is usually festooned with ribbons to indicate its symbolic aspect. It was popularly used as an ornamental element. It shows the animal's importance in ritual and observance to the gods. The bull was commonly sacrificed in ritual but was also a popular symbol of fertility. The bulcranium also became a popular motif in butcher's shops as an indication of their produce.

Astrology, Mysticism, and Myth

### Caduceus

This ancient symbol is a winged staff with two entwined serpents. The staff is the attribute of the Roman god Mercury and the Greek god Hermes—the messenger of the gods. Mercury was also considered the protector of merchants and traders. Consequently, the caduceus was adopted as the symbol of commerce and appears on many office buildings, including the great bronze doors of the Bank of England.

### Caryatid

Thought of as merely a decorative architectural device, caryatids actually record the unhappy plight of the Caryae women. According to Vitruvius's work of 1511, the Caryae were a people who lived in the Peloponnese and allied themselves to the Persians during their sporadic wars against the Greeks. After one particular Greek victory, the Caryae women were captured and enslaved and forced to work by carrying heavy burdens on their heads. The caryatid became a popular classical and neoclassical decoration.

### Centaur

With a man's head and torso and the body and legs of a horse, the centaur is a mythical "wild" beast and a symbol of barbarism for the ancient Greeks. Centaurs were supposed to become drunk and lecherous at the smallest drop of wine. During the Italian Renaissance centaurs came to symbolize man's bestial nature, especially in relation to abusing drink and violating women. The only exception was the immortal centaur Chiron, the gentle teacher and mentor of Achilles who was revered for his wisdom and humanity.

### Cupid

Cupid is the Roman god of love and symbolizes love in its many forms. He carries a quiver and bow and arrows with which to send his love darts. Sometimes he is shown blindfolded to portray the random nature of falling in love; when he looses a burning bolt it signifies the fires of passion. When Cupid is shown playing with weapons such as those belonging to Mars, it signifies the triumph of love over war and strife. Similarly, when shown with Father Time, he symbolizes the power of love to endure past the grave.

### Gorgon

The Gorgons of Greek mythology were three hideous and fearsome sisters whose look could turn a victim to stone. One of them, Medusa, was killed by Perseus. In symbolism a gorgon is shown as a female head with a horrifying expression, piercing eyes, hair of snakes, and sometimes wings in the hair; her tongue often pokes out of her mouth. The Gorgon was often placed at the entrance to Greek temples to ward off evil. It is also the Great Mother in her terrible and destructive aspect.

### Jupiter's staff

Jupiter's staff is a form of trident or fish spear but with three prongs at both ends. Jupiter was the warrior god guardian of Rome, the supreme god of the Roman pantheon of gods (Iuppiter Optimus Maximus), and the protector of youths. Known as Iuppiter he appeared in various forms; his best known aspects were as Iuppiter Conservator Orbis, the preserver of the world; Iuppiter Fulgur, the god of lightning; and Iuppiter Tonans, the god of thunder.

### Justice

This strong female symbol of judicial power is the personification of Justice, one of the Virtues. In a Renaissance addition to her aspect, she is shown blindfolded, representing the impartial administration of law. Justice holds a sword in one hand as her emblem of power, and in the other hand she holds the scales in which she will impartially weigh the cause she is called upon to judge. She is often shown as a statue above law courts.

### Lyre

This ancient instrument was played two and a half thousand years ago in ancient Mesopotamia; it would have been decorated with a bull's head. In classical times legend attributed the lyre as an invention of Hermes/Mercury, who, by putting bull sinews over the shell of a tortoise devised the instrument. He then gave the instrument to Apollo in exchange for a caduceus. The lyre and the caduceus then became the attributes of those respective gods. When Apollo played, the music was supposed to calm turmoil and trouble and inspire prophecies.

### Odin's cross

Odin's cross is an ancient pagan symbol representing the sun. The Vikings associated the sign with their supreme god, Odin, one of the three main gods in the Norse cosmos, along with Thor and Freyr. When the Vikings adopted Christianity, the symbol was easily incorporated into the Christian cross. Odin was not a warrior but a strategist who traveled far and wide on his eight-legged horse named Sleipnir. He was god of the dead and presided over banquets of those slain in battle. By drinking at Mimir's fountain, Odin became all-wise, but had to pledge one eye in return. His other eye is the sun.

### Odin's staff

Odin was the Norse father of gods and men and his name meant "inspirer of fury," as needed for battle. His staff symbolized his preeminence and also his power as a wandering magician. His staff also represented a wand. The three prongs at the top of the staff symbolize prosperity, power, and the number three—itself a symbol of magic. Odin is the god of knowledge, war, and most important, of victory. Assisted by his son, Thor, he directs the continual struggle against the forces of evil. He is the patron of all fighters killed honorably in battle.

### Rod of Aesculapius

Aesculapius is the Greek god of healing in whose shrines often lived sacred snakes. His rod is entwined by two serpents, one representing sickness and the other health; the rod has been symbolic of the medical profession since ancient times, when it indicated the location of a surgery or physician. In modern times it symbolizes medicine in general and is often found on drugstores and hospitals.

### Satyr

This mythological creature has a man's bearded head and torso, with the horns, hairy legs, cloven hoofs, and tail of a goat. Satyrs attend Bacchus, the god of revelry, and are often swathed in ropes of flowers and ivy leaves, and carry armfuls of fruit and pitchers of wine. They are fertility spirits but with a carnal and lustful aspect intent on hedonism, not procreation. They symbolized good crops, fertile flocks, and a good grape harvest. The demigod Pan was a satyr. By late medieval and Renaissance times they had come to symbolize evil, and Satan began to be depicted as a satyr.

### Staff of Poseidon

Poseidon was the Greek god of water. His staff is a trident, a traditional three-pronged fishing spear, the symbol of his authority over all matters aquatic. Poseidon, together with Apollo, built the walls of Troy, but on completion the Trojans betrayed him and refused to give him his reward. Consequently, he sided against Troy in the war. The trident is also the symbolic weapon against evil belonging to the Hindu god Shiva; its three prongs represent creation, preservation, and destruction.

### Thor's hammer

Thor's "hammer" was named Mjöllnir and was one of Thor's three precious objects (the others were his belt and iron gloves). It was the Norse symbol of lightning and masculine force. Thor rode across the sky in a chariot pulled in a roar of thunder and storm by two male goats. As he rides he brandishes Mjöllnir (actually a type of short-handled club), with which he strikes fear into the hearts of his enemies and crushes their skulls. It has the virtue of returning to him after it is thrown.

### Three Graces

Thalia, Euphrosyne, and Aglaia were attendants of Aphrodite/Venus and symbols of female beauty in the classical world. Their attributes were apple, myrtle, and rose. They always appear with arms linked, with two of them facing forward and the center figure facing inward. In Renaissance times they were taken to symbolize Beauty, Love, and Chastity, or, alternatively, the three stages of love—Beauty, Desire, and Fulfillment.

### Torch

For the ancient Greeks a torch was a symbol of life and by extension, when turned upside down and extinguished, became a symbol of death. A dead torch was often used on tombs and memorial statuary, and the Romans showed upside down torches being carried by cupids on the tombs of children. A flaming torch also signifies the fires of love and often is used as an attribute of Venus, Eros, and Hymen, the god of marriage.

### Victory

For the Greeks and Romans victory was personified as a winged female figure who carried a crown or laurel wreath for the victor and a palm leaf to symbolize victory in battle. The Greek goddess Nike was an aspect of Athena and was shown carrying a victor's laurel wreath and a globe. Before going into battle, Greek soldiers would sacrifice to her for success.

### Zeus

Zeus is the most important god in the Greek pantheon and he became the supreme civic god and protector of law and justice. His symbol is the thunderbolt, representing his lordship of weather, the skies, and the winds. His authority over the other gods and goddesses was based on power as symbolized by thunderbolts made for him by his armorers, the giant Cyclopes. Their workshop was under Mount Aetna and the smoke and flames of their furnaces can still be seen today.

# Religious Symbols

Religion and symbolism go hand in hand. To a greater degree than even politics, religion uses symbols to convey complex philosophical ideas and beliefs. Much religious symbolism grew out of the very earliest use of symbols, when mankind believed in the spirits of the elements—earth, wind, water, and fire. The universal elements are central to all beliefs and all manner of worship. As people became more sophisticated, these ideas became personified, and gods and goddesses became protectors and guardians of particular aspects of life and death.

When a new religion was imposed on an existing one, aspects of the old were often incorporated into the new, so that within a generation the old beliefs were largely forgotten. When Christianity was being established as the state religion in England, new festivals were imposed on the original heathen or pagan celebrations—thus Christmas, the celebration of the birth of Christ, was imposed on the ancient winter solstice celebrations; Easter imposed on the festival of Eostre at the spring equinox, and so on.

Many of the symbols shown here belong to the Christian tradition, but numerous early Christian symbols have a history that predates Christianity. It is interesting to see how popular elements—particularly birds and beasts—have been incorporated into Christian iconography.

In addition to the manifold symbols of Christianity, crosses from all parts of the Christian world have become identified with a particular branch or region of the religion. Crosses were commonly used in heraldry, in a wide variety of ornamentally stylized shapes and forms. They were particularly chosen for coats of arms by people going on crusade.

### Apocalypse

Belief in the Apocalypse—the imminent second coming of Christ—was the belief that sustained early Christians when they were persecuted by the Romans. The Apocalypse was a vision of John the Evangelist's. There are many versions of his vision, but this symbol shows his instruction to teach his beliefs to the seven Christian communities in Asia Minor (the seven "lamps") and the enthroned Christ with eyes aflame and a sword emerging from his mouth. John is the figure often depicted crouching beside him.

### Apocalyptic lamb

The newborn lamb was the unfortunate sacrificial beast in many old religions. The Apocalyptic lamb was adopted as a metaphor to signify how good was destined to overcome evil and sin—it was used as a symbol of the teachings of Christ defeating the evils of ignorance and darkness. Christ was often represented as a lamb—an animal of complete innocence and purity—and in early Christian art the Apostles were frequently shown as twelve sheep surrounding the Lamb of God.

### Bleeding heart

In Roman Catholic iconography the bleeding heart symbolizes the Virgin Mary and shows the terrible sorrow she suffered when her son died on the cross. The bleeding heart is also symbolic of the suffering of Christ. When the heart appears pierced by three nails under a crown of thorns, it symbolically refers to Christ's crucifixion.

### Chrismon

This double cross is known as a Chrismon or Christ sign. This very early Christian symbol is a combination of the Latin cross and the Greek "X" cross and is one of the monograms of Christ.

### Christian fish

These days the sign of the fish represents Christianity, but the history of this symbol goes back much further than the age of Christ to pagan times, where it was used as a fertility awareness icon. Other cultures also use the shape of the fish to signify reincarnation and the life force. In Greek mythology, Ichthys was the son of the sea goddess Atargatis, and in certain dialects his name meant "womb" or "dolphin" —this led to early depictions of mermaids. The fish symbol was also used by many other early cultures, including associations with the goddess of Ephesus and the Egyptian god Osiris.

### Christian symbol for victory

The Christian symbol for the triumph of good over evil is a Latin cross surmounted by a stylized crown. This symbol was used in the early days of the church when Christianity was a radical religious movement and the battle was very real. Later it came to symbolize the triumph of God over death, and can also mean the ultimate victory on the day of the Lord when all creation will be made new.

### Doom

The symbol of Doom, or the Last Judgment, was a popular subject of Christian iconography used to encourage church morality among the masses. It symbolized the separation of the saved from the damned and the righteous from the unrighteous. The symbol shows an angel with the Last Trumpet calling mankind to account for its sins. It was intended to arouse visions of damnation in the minds of potential sinners and encourage them with the lure of heavenly rewards.

### Door

Symbolic of beginnings and endings and the crossing point between one life and the next, doors have great significance in many cultures. For ancient Egyptians the door was a symbol for both entry and defense. Doors leading into temples and tombs were guarded by lions or mythical beasts, and the door to the netherworld was guarded by fire-spitting serpents. In many religions the opening of temple or shrine doors symbolizes the opening of the gates of heaven.

### Five sacred wounds

This symbol, dating from the late Middle Ages, celebrates the sacrificial love that Jesus Christ proved through his crucifixion on Mount Calvary. The symbol shows the wounds Christ suffered when nails were driven through his hands and feet, the spear that cut his torso, his heart, and the crown of thorns that the Roman soldiers placed on his head. At the time, Christian spirituality stressed the very human agony that the incarnate God endured for mankind.

111

### Gnostic sun

The Gnostics were an early mystical Christian sect dating from the end of the first century A.D. who claimed that matter was evil, denying that Christ had existed in corporeal form as a man. They believed in salvation through secret knowledge or gnosis. This symbol represents the sun with the crossbars at the ends representing the vault of the heavens. The established church saw Gnostics as peddling a dangerously heretical perversion of Christianity.

### Lamb

The Paschal Lamb, or Agnus Dei, is one of the oldest symbols of Christ, as the lamb was used as the pure and innocent victim in many ritual sacrifices. The lamb symbolizes Jesus' sacrifice for mankind on the cross and alludes to the Jewish Passover that traditionally involves the sacrifice of a lamb. The Lamb of God is shown standing on a hill from which four streams of weather flow—these represent the Christian church and the four gospels.

### Lamb and flag

The lamb lying down with a flag supported by its foreleg is the emblem of the prophet St. John the Baptist. The lamb is symbolic of innocence, and sorcerers are powerless against them. When shown with a flag or pennant, the lamb is symbolic of the resurrection. For the symbol of St. John the Baptist the lamb and flag signify that he is the forerunner of Christ.

### Lechery

One of the seven deadly sins, lechery is a vice associated with lust. Old Christian teaching not only symbolized and personified the sins but also gave the antidote: to say the Lord's Prayer, meditate on the instruments of the Passion, and, in the case of lust, appeal to Susanna. She was malevolently accused of adultery by two elderly would-be lovers and subsequently tried in court; Daniel defended her and proved her innocence. Other symbols of lust include centaurs, mermaids, and swine.

### Menorah

This seven-branched candelabra is one of the most ancient symbols of Judiasm. It is thought to be a stylized version of the Tree of Life, and for Jews it represents the light of God and judgment. It is often used on the entrance to synagogues and schools and now has an official capacity as the emblem of Israel. The menorah is used at Hanukkah, the Jewish winter festival of lights.

### Monogram of Jesus

Originally the monogram was IHC, the first three letters of the name Jesus in Greek. Then it was changed to read IHS, for the Latin *in hoc signo,* meaning "in this sign." Other interpretations read "Jesus hominum Salvator," meaning "Jesus redeemer of mankind." The cross above the letters is symbolic of his suffering on the cross.

### Pelican

In medieval Christian bestiaries (books that describe animals both real and imaginary, which were used for moral teaching) the mother pelican is shown piercing her breast to feed her young on her own blood. In this aspect the pelican was believed to echo Christ's work, in particular his sacrifice and resurrection. This image was especially popular in the thirteenth century, by which time it represented redemption, sacrifice, and atonement.

### Scallop shell

The scallop shell became a pilgrims' symbol of their journey to a holy shrine. The usage originated in the twelfth century, with pilgrims traveling to the shrine of St. James of Compostela in northern Spain. They used his symbol, a scallop shell, on their clothing and bags to indicate their journey. The scallop shell quickly came to indicate any pilgrimage. Pilgrims would drill a pair of holes through the flat end so the shell could be suspended from a leather thong.

### Seal of the world

This symbol comes from the Gnostic mystical tradition, from a heritage that probably predates Christianity. Gnosticism was strong in the second century when its teachings threatened the stability of the Christian church. Little is known about the Gnostics except that they were followers of a variety of religious movements who believed in salvation through gnosis. Gnostics tended to be radical ascetics who considered women the source of evil and children as souls in bondage to the powers of darkness.

### Signum Dei

Also called the chi-rho, this is probably the best known symbol of Christ, and may even be older than the cross as a Christian symbol. The symbol is composed of the two Greek initial letters of the name Christ, "X" and "P." In legend this appeared in a dream to Emperor Constantine (c. A.D. 274–337): he heard a voice saying, "In this sign shalt thou conquer." Constantine then ordered the sign emblazoned on his war banner, which was called the Labarum.

### St. John

St. John's symbol is an eagle that soars unerringly to the sun of divinity. John is the attributed author of the fourth Gospel, which was probably written in Ephesus—at the time a center for religious debate where Jews and Christians could meet and discuss theological issues. There is some mystery about the author; some sources say that it is John the Apostle, while others maintain that it was another John who lived to a great age in Ephesus and probably died there.

### St. Luke

St. Luke's symbol is a winged ox that alludes to the sacrifice of Zacharias. The epistles record that St. Luke was a physician as well as the companion of St. Paul. He was a Greek gentile who probably came from Antioch. He lived a generation later than Jesus and is the reputed author of the third Gospel as well as of the Acts of the Apostles. He was not an eyewitness to the events surrounding Jesus but gathered together stories and anecdotes and used the Gospel of St. Mark as the basis for his work.

### St. Mark

St. Mark's symbol is a winged lion and alludes to a voice crying in the wilderness. St. Mark's Gospel was the first to be written and is the shortest. Both Matthew and Luke used his work as the basis for their gospels.

St. Mark traveled to Rome as St. Peter's companion; it is possible that he wrote the gospel there, having gotten much of his information firsthand from St. Peter. His symbol has been depicted in Venice since A.D. 829, when his putative remains were interred in the patriarchal church there.

### St. Matthew

St. Matthew's symbol shows Christ as a winged man, alluding to the time he spent on earth in the guise of a man. Originally believed to be the Apostle Matthew, this Matthew is now thought to be a Greek-speaking Jew from Syria. Matthew's Gospel is the first book of the New Testament; however, scholars concur that he used the earlier Gospel of St. Mark as the basis for his enlarged and extended version.

### Star of David

Also known as Magen David. This six-pointed star composed of two equilateral triangles first became a Judaic symbol in the twelfth century and since then has become synonymous with Jews and the state of Israel. It replaced the menorah as the emblem of Judaism in the sixteenth century.

### The Blessed Sacrament

In Christian worship, the sacrament of the Eucharist is the high point of worship. The symbol for the blessed sacrament shows a chalice with a circular host—often embossed with a crucifix or the IHS monogram—appearing from the bowl. The wafer is consecrated by the officiating priest to become the body, soul, and divinity of Christ, and the wine his blood, as Jesus commanded at the Last Supper.

### Vishnu

This is the symbol for Vishnu, the Hindu god of love. The stories of Vishnu's life are legion, and he appears in many different aspects, including a fish, a boar, a turtle, a dwarf, and a lion-man. He is a solar god who lives in the heavens and who was said to have crossed the universe in three strides. As the principle of the light that penetrates the entire universe, he is the conqueror of darkness. His friends and companions are the Maruts, the gods of storm and air.

### Canterbury

The Archbishop of Canterbury is the premier bishop in the Church of England. This cross is used by the Archbishop of Canterbury as a symbol of his position. It is used to surmount his staff. The shape of this cross is termed cross formée. Crosses in a variety of ornamentally stylized shapes are often used in heraldic devices.

### Celtic

Also called High Crosses,
Celtic crosses are ancient,
elaborately decorated crosses
with carvings in Celtic
interlaced-knotwork style.
They date from around the
tenth century. Many are still
found scattered around the
countryside in Ireland
and southwest England,
particularly in Cornwall. The
designs on the crosses vary
according to their age and
where they were carved, but
they are always distinguished
by a circle surrounding the
intersection of the cross and
elaborate, often highly
sophisticated, decoration.

### Consecrated church

This is an old sign often found
on old Roman Catholic
churches, either carved into
the stone near the entrance or
painted on the walls. It shows
that the church has been
consecrated and is sacred
to God.

### Coptic cross

The Coptic (Christian) church
in Egypt uses this cross. The
symbol represents the cross
on which Jesus was crucified,
and the four *T*s surrounding
it symbolize the four nails
with which Jesus was nailed
to the cross.

### Cross Four-Fs

The cross in many variations is an ancient motif. This German cross is made up of four *F*s, which stand for *frisch, fromm, frölich,* and *frei:* strong, God-fearing, cheerful, and free.

### Fleurée

The cross fleurée, or fleury, has narrow limbs that terminate in stylized floral ends, which curl outward and resemble a sort of fleur-de-lis or flower form. As a more ornamental version of the Greek cross, it is popularly used in heraldry.

### Globical

This is a fuller version of the cross fleurée and is occasionally used as a shape for ornaments and medals. It is typical of the variety of styles that the basic cross shape is used for. The globical cross is similar in shape to an Iron Cross (see page 129) except that the ends of the cross legs are convex rather than straight. The globical cross provides the base shape for the Canterbury cross, without the latter's elaborate decoration on the legs.

### Greek

All four arms of the Greek cross are the same length. It is one of the simplest symbols and since ancient times has been used to represent different things. In ancient Greece it represented the four elements—earth, air, fire, and water. In the ancient Middle East the same symbol was used to represent the four cardinal directions—north, south, east, and west—and the four winds. It is also used in Buddhism to represent two crossed thunderbolts, which show the power of Buddha's wisdom; it is called *visra vajra* and represents a Buddhist ritual implement. In Aztec mythology such a cross represents a meeting place or crossroads sacred to the god Yacatecutli ("Lord Nose").

### Iona

The Iona cross differs from the Celtic cross by having widened ends to the arms. The small island of Iona is in the Inner Hebrides, off the northern coast of Scotland. In A.D. 563, St. Columba landed on the island and started the Christianization of Scotland. He made the island his headquarters and stayed there for thirty-four years while he carried out his mission. Iona became a place of pilgrimage and veneration and ever since has had strong religious associations. Later a Benedictine community was founded there. Kings of Scotland, Ireland, and Norway were buried there in tribute to Iona's holiness.

### Jerusalem

Also known as the cross potent or the crusader's cross. The ends of this cross terminate in potents or crutches. In the space between the arms sit four smaller crosses, which some interpreters see as symbolizing the five wounds of Christ. The cross of Jerusalem was used in the insignia of the Kingdom of Jerusalem when it was established by the crusaders in the Middle Ages.

### Latin

Also known as Crux ordinaria, the Passion cross, or Long cross, this represents the cross on which Jesus Christ was crucified and is a holy symbol for Christians. It is considered the sign of all signs, and many other crosses are versions of this. When this cross sits on three steps it is called the Calvary cross or Holy cross. The three steps are symbolic of the three Christian graces of faith, hope, and charity. Significantly, the top and side arms of the Latin cross are the same length. The earliest known example is from fourth century Rome.

### Maltese

This cross has eight points or ends. The Knights of Malta used a form of this cross on their badge, as did some other religious orders. Supposedly the eight points of the cross represent the eight beatitudes (blessings). Furthermore, when the order of knights was created, it was overseen and guided by eight powerful European states: Germany, England, Italy, France, Provence, Auvergne, Castile, and Aragon.

### Papal

This triple cross is used by the Pope as one of his symbols of office. The Pope, also known as the Bishop of Rome, is the global head of the Roman Catholic Church and is regarded as the successor of St. Peter. The Pope is elected by the college of cardinals of which he is a member until his elevation. Since the First Vatican Council his pronouncements on matters of faith have been regarded by Roman Catholics as infallible. He remains in office until his death.

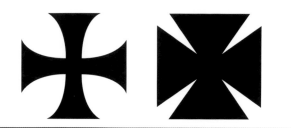

### Patée

This old cross shape was favored by early Christians and is often found carved into ancient Christian buildings. With this cross the limbs are narrow at the center and gradually expand and then curve outward into the ends to finish in a flat cut. It is often used as a shape for medals and ornamentation.

### Patée formée

This is very similar to the plain patée cross but is much fuller and fatter in its form. This shape is popularly chosen for medals since it gives more room for inscriptions and decoration than other crosses.

### Patriarchal

This is also known as the Cross of Lorraine. It has two horizontal bars, with the lower longer than the upper; the upper, shorter bar represents the titulus with the inscription "INRI" that was fixed by order of Pontius Pilate over Jesus Christ. It gets its name from the legend that the ancient patriarchs of Jerusalem bore this cross. The patriarchs were the five bishops of the sees of medieval Christendom. The patriarchal cross was later adopted by successive patriarchs of Constantinople.

### Roman sacred cross

This more elaborate cross is of Roman origin. The cross has become one of the main symbols of Christianity, and of Jesus Christ in particular, even though it represents an instrument of horrific torture that inflicts a long, slow, and painful death. It is an example of the way the cross has been elaborated to such an extent that its original function is almost completely lost.

### Russian Orthodox

This is a further adaptation of the patriarchal cross, with a lower skewed slat that represents the board to which Christ's feet were nailed. Such crosses are often seen on the domed tops of Russian Orthodox churches. The Russian Orthodox church has been the principal church of Russia since 988; in Soviet times it was repressed and followers discouraged, but since the fall of the Soviet Union, membership of the Russian Orthodox Church has increased.

### St. Andrew's

Also known as a saltire. In the late Middle Ages the story arose that this was the form of cross that St. Andrew was crucified on at Patras (Patrae) in Achaia on November 30, A.D. 60. St. Andrew was a Galilean fisherman and the brother of Simon Peter, with whom he was fishing when Jesus asked him to become one of his disciples. The saltire's most familiar use is on the flag and in the arms of Scotland.

### St. Peter's

This cross is used as the symbol of St. Peter, one of Jesus' first disciples. St. Peter was a Galilean fisherman before he became one of Jesus' disciples. When Jesus was being tried, Peter denied knowing him three times, but he later repented his denials. After Jesus' death Peter traveled around the Mediterranean preaching the word of Christ. He is known to have visited Corinth and probably lived his last days in Rome, where he is reputed to be buried.

### Tau cross

For Christians this is known as the Tau cross, but it is also the Egyptian symbol of life, the Key of the Nile.

### Trefly

Also known as a cross botonée, related to the French word *bouton,* meaning "knob" or "bud." This is another variant on the standard cross, but here the ends of the cross terminate in three lobes, like a trefoil leaf.

# Politics and Power

Politicians love symbols—as in religion, a simple drawing can sum up complex ideas and philosophies. Every modern political party has a symbol through which it hopes to express its ethos. Some of these symbols have historical precedent, but most are modern concoctions devised for instant recognition. Accordingly, many of them disappear into obscurity once the political momentum has stopped.

Symbols have long been used to express hatred and solidarity against a particular (though usually nonspecified) enemy. The most obvious symbol of hate is the Nazi swastika still used to signify fascism and other unsavory elements promulgated by the Nazi party in Germany in the 1930s and 1940s. This is an abuse of an antique symbol that was probably a positive sun sign—no one knows for sure because its use is so ancient. Adolf Hitler is said to have deliberately chosen the swastika for its aura of good omen but mistakenly positioned it rotating clockwise instead of the more usual counterclockwise.

Activists of all persuasions use symbols, and today they can easily become fashion icons. On badges and T-shirts, symbols provide a useful shorthand of a whole range of political concepts, tendencies, and allegiances. They signal like-minded people to each other and also signify people you might like to avoid. Symbols of power and politics are the most transitory of all, appearing suddenly and then, as social politics move on, disappearing completely.

### Anarchy

The symbol for anarchy is the letter "A" with a circle drawn around it. There are many anarchist organizations, varying from those who want a simple life without the existence of a national government to those who seek to propagate violence and the disintegration of society. The original tenet of anarchy is that society should be reorganized into small, self-determining communities with common ownership of land and produce, so that individual liberty and equality may prevail.

### Anti-ANC South African

This South African symbol from the apartheid era is the sign for the Afrikaaner Weerstandsbeweging, a white supremacist organization that supported the apartheid laws. In particular, the organization opposed the African National Congress (ANC) and all attempts to end segregation. Afrikaners were originally Europeans who were born in the Dutch Cape Colony in South Africa; they are also known as Boers (meaning "farmers" in Dutch). Afrikaners were the dominant force in South African politics until the 1990s.

### Democrat donkey

This unofficial symbol of the Democratic Party originated as an insult hurled at Andrew Jackson when he was running for president in 1828. He was called a jackass by his opponents for expounding populist views, but he cleverly took advantage of the ensuing publicity by using the jackass on his campaign posters. The donkey came to symbolize him and later the Democratic Party. This solidified when the political cartoonist Thomas Nast satirized American politics and the anti–Civil War faction (Democrats) as a donkey in an 1870 issue of *Harper's Weekly*. By 1880 the donkey had become a mascot for the party as a symbol of a clever and courageous animal.

### Donnerkeil/thunderbolt

*Donnerkeil* is German for "thunderbolt." Also known as "Sig-rune ähnlich," this symbol is a variation of the victory rune. It was used by the Dutch Nazi party and the British Nazi party as an indication of their fascist beliefs.

### Double-headed eagle

The double-headed eagle first made its appearance on Hittite reliefs and then on Indian coinage, but was not seen in Europe until the Crusades. With outstretched wings symbolizing perpetual watchfulness, it was adopted as the emblem of the Holy Roman Empire. When the empire collapsed in 1805, the eagle survived to be used by the Austro-Hungarian Empire as a symbol of their might and all-encompassing power. Sometimes the eagle holds a crown in its beak, which symbolizes immortality.

### German anarchy

This adaptation of the more familiar anarchy graffiti symbol was first recorded at Sassnitz in Germany during the early 1990s. Instead of conveying the formal concept of anarchy—a condition in which people live in harmony together without written laws—this symbol is a call for aggression, disorder, chaos, and direct confrontation with the law. Such anarchist movements were a response by some disenfranchised members of society to the blatant consumerism of the 1980s.

### German squatter sign

This sign was used by an anarchistic German youth movement who confronted police and authorities and challenged the intent to demolish habitable housing in order to rebuild with expensive high-rise buildings. Squatting or house-occupying became prevalent in the late twentieth century, when house prices and rents made permanent homes an impossibility for many people. At the same time, the economy made property a lucrative source of income for developers and speculators.

### Imperial eagle

The Roman Empire was pictured in the form of an eagle with outspread wings, which symbolized its all-encompassing power and ultimate victory over its enemies. In 1804, centuries after the fall of the Roman Empire, the French emperor Napoleon Bonaparte adopted the eagle as his military emblem to show his and France's strength. His eagle was shown surrounded by a laurel wreath of victory, and was a deliberate reference to the lasting power and influence of the Roman Empire.

### Iron Cross

The Iron Cross was initiated by King Friedrich Wilhelm III of Prussia in 1813 as an award for bravery during the War of Liberation. However, it has come to be indelibly associated with the Germany Nazi regime during the 1930s and 1940s. It was the only major decoration awarded by the Nazis that existed before the Third Reich era. In 1939, when Hitler first started awarding the cross, it had four grades, with officers getting higher grades than soldiers; this was increased to eight grades by 1945. The Iron Cross was also awarded to civilians in recognition of their bravery—police, fire, and railroad servicemen were all eligible.

### Ku Klux Klan

This name probably derives from the Greek *kyklos,* meaning circle. The Ku Klux Klan (KKK) first appeared in the South after the Civil War (1861–1865), when it was founded to oppose reconstruction, especially the new rights granted to blacks. Disguised under white hoods and robes, Klan members spread terror, including grotesque lynchings. Federal laws reduced its effect until the early 1900s; it died out in the 1940s, but revived in the '60s due to increased civil rights activities. The late twentieth century found its membership severely reduced.

### League of Arab States

The crescent is synonymous with Islamic culture, and this version of the horizontal crescent is the symbol of the League of Arab States, an informal association of predominantly Arabic-speaking sovereign states. Initially suggested by Egypt in 1943, the league was formed by seven Arab countries in 1945 with the intention of strengthening ties and promoting their mutual interests in politics, economic, cultural, and social programs. Since then the number of member countries has increased.

### Nazi German eagle

The Nazi eagle is a stylized bird with its head turned to its right and very linear outstretched wings. In its claws it holds a wreath in the center of which sits a swastika. The eagle—heavy with the symbolism of the might of the Roman Empire and the historic German imperial eagle—was an obvious choice for the Nazis' principal symbol (alongside the swastika). The eagle was extensively used on badges and insignia, and for huge statues on top of buildings and monuments.

### Nazi SS runes

The Nazis used a lot of symbolism in their many political and military organizations. One of the most infamous military units was the Schutzstaffel, also known as the "SS," whose members were notoriously ruthless. Some worked for the Gestapo, others in the many German death camps. The most famous of their many insignia are the SS runes, also known as bolts or lightning strikes, which were worn as collar patches. These came from the Sig rune, which was an ancient Germanic symbol for Thor, the god of thunder. Today it is often seen in association with white supremacist groups, and in neo-Nazi tattoos and graffiti.

### Nazi swastika

Adolf Hitler and the Nazi (National Socialist) Party adopted the clockwise rotating swastika as their official emblem because of its ancient good luck omens and positive symbology; since that time it has become associated with evil. During World War II, the Nazis used the swastika as their predominant symbol, on everything from buildings to stamps. Since their demise the swastika has been used by racist groups to signify hate, in particular against followers of the Jewish faith.

### Peace

The symbol for the Campaign for Nuclear Disarmament (CND) was designed in 1958, and has since become known as the peace symbol or "Ban the Bomb." The shape comes from the semaphore letters N and D (for "nuclear" and "disarmament") within a circle, which represents global unity. The CND was formed as a direct result of the horror felt by people all over the world after the death and destruction wrought by the atomic bombs dropped on Hiroshima and Nagasaki. Initially there were many similar groups, but the CND became the largest and most influential.

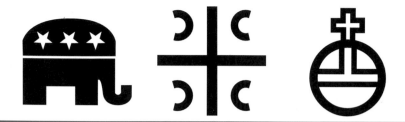

### Republican elephant

The official symbol of the Republican Party came about thanks to the political cartoonist Thomas Nast— who was also largely responsible for the Democrat donkey—when he drew Republican supporters as an elephant in a satirical cartoon for *Harper's Weekly* in 1874. In a cartoon entitled "Third Term Panic" (President Ulysses S. Grant was running for a third term), he showed the donkey disguised in a lion's skin, attempting to scare away all the animals in the woods (a reference to the animals in the zoo in Central Park). The cowering elephant carried a sign saying "The Republican Vote."

### Serbian graffiti

This symbol was commonly seen as graffiti in the Balkans during the ethnic wars in the former Yugoslavia in the early 1990s. The symbol is a much simplified version of the coat of arms of Serbia—one of the main protagonists in the ethnic conflict. Serbia was founded in the sixth century but was conquered by the Turks in the late fourteenth century. The conquest lasted until the late nineteenth century. Independent for a short time, Serbs united with Croats and Slovenes in 1918; they then became Yugoslavia in 1929.

### Sign of the Byzantine emperors

This sign is a collective symbol of two important indicators of power and was used as the symbol for the all-powerful Byzantine emperor. The orb is a euphemism for the globe, and was used by Roman emperors to show their dominance over the known world. The symbol at the top represented the goddess of victory, but when the emperor Constantine (c. A.D. 280–337) converted to Christianity, this was replaced by a cross to symbolize that the Byzantine Empire was a Christian power.

### Viva!

This simple symbol stands for greeting and exultation, as in "hail!" or "hurrah!" It was used in a political context to urge on victory, particularly when an election was pending. Conversely, when turned upside down, the sign means the exact opposite, as in "down with." This symbol is particularly popular in Italy to indicate political support and opposition.

### White power

The "White Power" fist, otherwise known as the "Aryan Fist," is a symbol derived from the fist representing the Black Power movement. The term *white power* is used by white supremacist organizations such as the American Nazi Party, who differ from the original Nazis in that they deny the holocaust ever happened and have incorporated religion into their fascist ideology. Nazism itself was mainly atheistic, although there were adherents of paganism and occultism present in the party. White Power today stands for the creation of an Aryan master race through a mix of racism and fascism.

# Symbols from the Western Tradition

Since before recorded history, symbols have been used as a form of shorthand to record and convey an often vast and complex range of meanings. Before most people could read, such symbols contributed an important subtext to monuments, records, buildings, and paintings of important personal and civic events. In the Western tradition, many symbols take the form of familiar plants, animals, and objects that have become imbued with particular and specific meanings.

Our ancestors could understand these signs and symbols, but in modern times their rich meanings have been forgotten. Yet many of us unconsciously "read" symbols without even thinking about it—roses and hearts mean love, and doves symbolize peace. Many symbols are not consistent in appearance and are often interpreted differently by artists, depending on their style and era; however, the meaning of the symbol will remain the same.

The histories and meanings of symbols are as fascinating as they are varied, and it would be a great shame if their significance were forgotten. Look at almost any memorial and symbols will be there; look at important civic buildings as well as less worthy structures—often a clear indication of the building's purpose is given in the symbols incorporated into the decoration.

### Britannia

Britannia is the feminine personification of the British Isles. The first representations of this symbol are on second century A.D. Romano-British coins. Britannia is based on the goddess Minerva, the Roman goddess of wisdom and patroness of arts and trades. She wears a Minervan helmet and holds a trident—a symbol of her power over the oceans—and a large oval shield that bears the Union Jack. She appeared in this form starting in 1665 and became the symbol of the British Empire, used on everything from coins to buildings.

### Dwarf

In European legend, dwarfs are generally used to symbolize the malign and amoral forces of nature who live in darkness in holes and caves in the earth. In Norse legend, four dwarfs support the sky at the corners of the earth. In India, Shiva, the god of the cosmic dance, is shown resting his foot on a dwarf, which symbolizes human ignorance. Vishnu, the Hindu god of love, in one legend appeared as a dwarf called Vamana in whose form he tricked the demon Bali into giving him the earth.

### Green Man

The Green Man is a mysterious ancient depiction that symbolizes the power and wildness of nature, plants, and the season of fall. It is always a male face half hidden by greenery and fronds that seem to be growing out of his mouth and sometimes out of his ears and eyes. His face was always flesh colored; it is the foliage around him that is green. He is most familiar from twelfth-century English churches, but was also a popular image across the Roman Empire from the Rhine to Turkey. In Turkey, the foliage was often acanthus leaves; in England, oak and hawthorn were most common.

### Liberty

Now synonymous with freedom and used as the emblem of the United States, the symbol of Liberty goes back to the Renaissance, when she was an important figure alongside her sisters Plenty, Peace, and Justice. They were used as effigies on administrative and official buildings to show the integrity of law and good government. Liberty's attributes are the Phrygian bonnet (freedom from oppression), a scepter (authority), and a flaming torch (the fire of love). Liberty became associated with revolution from oppression.

### Lion

The lion, "king of beasts," symbolizes power, pride, courage, and victory, and is an ancient and popular image used around the world to symbolize different strengths. In Islamic and Egyptian mythology, the lion protects against evil and was used to guard doorways and gates from the enemy. For ancient Greeks the lion symbolized remembrance of dead warriors; in early Christian iconography it symbolized Christ's resurrection. Another Christian belief was that the lion slept with open eyes — it was thus used as a symbol of spiritual watchfulness and vigilance. Many royal and imperial powers have used the lion as a symbol of their might.

### Marianne

The personification of France and symbol of the "Triumph of the Republic" is Marianne, an allegorical figure of Liberty and the Republic. Her image is seen on stamps, banknotes, and medals, and her bust sits in every town hall, *mairie* (mayor's office), and courtroom in France. Her origins are unclear, but she became associated with the French Revolution as a beautiful young woman who fought on the barricades and nursed the wounded *sans-culottes*. Over her long flowing hair she usually wears a Phrygian bonnet, a symbol of liberty worn by freed slaves in Greece and Rome and adopted by activists in the south of France during the Revolution.

135

### Uncle Sam

Uncle Sam is the informal personification of the U.S.A. Samuel Wilson (1766–1854) of Massachusetts, a soldier in the Revolutionary War, was the inspiration for Uncle Sam. After the war he moved to New York and built up a thriving meat packing business; he was nicknamed "Uncle Sam" due to his fair business dealings. In the War of 1812 he supplied meat to the army, stamping the boxes "U.S."—for U.S. army use only—before "U.S." was commonly used for "United States." Soon anything with a U.S. stamp was dubbed as coming from Uncle Sam. Political cartoonists dressed him patriotically in red, white, and blue, and gave him a Lincolnesque appearance.

### Albatross

The albatross travels alone across the great oceans of the world in tireless flight. For sailors it symbolized the coming of bad weather and high winds; they also believed the albatross embodied the soul of a dead sailor, so it was extremely unlucky to kill one as it would certainly bring down a curse on their ship. For the Ainu people of north Japan, the albatross is a sacred bird that is an omen of good fortune in its role as the most important servant of the chief god of the sea.

### American eagle

The American eagle is clearly the indigenous great bald eagle that wafts over the great plains of America. As a symbol it is nevertheless depicted in classical style, with outstretched wings and turned head. It is used on the dollar bill as well as on many official seals and insignia. It usually appears with a striped shield in front of its body and sometimes a halo of stars or a narrow, starred ribbon in its beak. The American eagle is often shown clutching an olive branch (peace) in one talon and an arrow (willingness to fight) in the other.

### Ass

The ass is a beast of burden and a mode of transportation for poor peoples in all cultures, so it is traditionally symbolic of poverty. The nature of the beast as stubborn and slow is also used as a metaphor for intractability. The ass features prominently in the Bible and was instrumental in carrying Mary and Joseph to Nazareth and Jesus to Jerusalem. For the Greeks the meaning was quite different: an ass was the mount of the satyr Silenus, and therefore it was associated with licentiousness and depravity.

### Basilisk

This mythical creature, also known as the cockatrice, symbolizes exceptional evil. A basilisk has the body of a snake and the crested head and feathered legs and claws of a rooster. In medieval Christian lore, the basilisk was thought to be an aspect of the devil in his form as the king of the serpents. It was believed to kill with a single venomous glance and to expel fatally poisonous breath. However, a basilisk could be killed if it was tricked into looking at itself in a mirror.

### Bee

Bees are symbolic of hard work, industry, and the common good. For the ancient Chinese and Greeks bees also symbolize immortality and rebirth. In Chinese art, a bee hovering over a flower symbolizes a lady being courted by a man. In the nineteenth century, the worker bee was adopted as the symbol of self-help groups, in particular the cooperative movement. When shown flying around a hive, bees symbolize eloquence; they have been used on memorials to great speakers as an allusion to "honeyed words."

### Bull

As a powerful, imposing beast, the bull symbolizes strength and masculinity as well as fertility. In ancient times, bulls were often associated with solar and sky gods and depicted as the consort of the Mother Goddess. Bulls were worshiped in the eastern Mediterranean, Egypt, Crete, and the ancient Near East, as well as in classical Greece and Rome. In some cultures bulls were sacrificial animals, slaughtered to appease the gods and ensure a good harvest. In the cult of Dionysus/Bacchus, the devotees ripped a bull apart and ate its flesh raw, releasing the god's power and passing it on to his followers.

### Crane

Used by the Romans as the symbol of vigilance and watchfulness. These attributes came from a legend, recorded by Aristotle, in which a crane was described as standing on one foot and holding a stone in its raised other claw; if the bird fell asleep it would drop the stone and wake itself up. In China, the crane was revered as the messenger of the gods. In Japan, the crane was an emblem symbolizing happiness and prosperity.

### Dog

Dogs are faithful to their masters, and in most cultures are symbols of faithfulness, loyalty, and often of hunting. To Native American Lakota people, their spirits bring faithfulness, while for Maoris dogs symbolize departed spirits who guard the tribe from danger. Zoroastrians entrust the dog to guide and protect the departed soul while it journeys to the next world. In Western mythology, dogs represent marital fidelity on the tombs of beloved wives; if the dog is chained it represents the confines of marriage.

### Dolphin

The dolphin is a much-loved mammal and was the symbol of Apollo and an attribute of Poseidon/Neptune. Dolphins symbolize the sea and were commonly used in the emblems of maritime cities. It was a popular emblem for the Etruscans, and many cultures have considered it to be the king of fish. Dolphins were used extensively on ancient mosaics and are depicted on Roman sarcophagi; these funereal dolphins are called "psychopomps." Early Christians used the symbol of the dolphin while Christianity was still an underground religion. When shown with a ship or anchor it came to represent Christ as the savior of souls and bearer of souls over the waters of death.

### Dove

The modern symbol of peace, the dove is actually an ancient symbol of love and an important attribute of the Roman goddess of love, Venus. Doves are a symbol of fidelity, as they are thought to take only one mate for life; at one time they became accomplices of Cupid's. For Christians the dove is a symbol of the Holy Spirit and innocence, and for that reason became closely associated with the ceremony of baptism.

### Dove of peace

A dove holding an olive branch in its beak is a very early Christian symbol of peace. This image was used in the Roman catacombs and meant "May you rest in peace." The dove and olive branch originates in the Old Testament story of Noah's ark, in which a dove flew back to the ark with an olive branch, indicating that land was nearby. The artist Pablo Picasso was so affected by World War II that he designed a poster featuring a white dove for the World Peace Congress, held in Paris in 1949.

### Duck

Equally at home on the water or in the sky, the duck is the mediator between affairs of the waters and sky for many Native American cultures. For the Chinese and Japanese ducks symbolize happiness. A pair of Mandarin ducks (*yuan-yang* in Chinese and *oshi-dori* in Japanese) symbolize conjugal happiness and fidelity, due to the belief that ducks and drakes mate for life. A Chinese lucky token to ward off accidents shows a duck sitting on a lotus, known as the Sacred Duck.

### Eagle

Known as the king of the birds. For the Assyrians a symbol of power and victory. The eagle is an attribute of Jupiter, the most powerful of the Roman gods, and of his Greek counterpart Zeus. Disguised as an eagle, Zeus carried off Ganymede, the most beautiful of all mortals. The Romans were fond of the eagle and used one with outspread wings as a symbol of strength on the standards of their legions.

### Eagle and serpent

The fighting eagle and snake originates in Sumeria and symbolizes the conflict between the sky and earth gods. The theme was taken up, with regional variations, by the ancient Greeks and in Hindu myth. For ancient Christians the image of an eagle fighting a serpent is symbolic of spiritual victory over the temptations of sin. For later Christians the eagle has become an attribute of St. John the Evangelist, hence its popular use as the main feature of lecterns in church.

### Fox

The fox is an animal found all over the world and consequently has many associations. The Celts believed that foxes were familiars of the devil and could transmute into witches. Similarly, for early Christians they symbolized the cunning of the devil, deception, and heresy. Medieval Christians liked to use the fox as a satirical figure, for example as a priest or judge. In Asia foxes are revered as the holders of the secrets of nature, and they were even worshiped as bearers of wealth. They were also thought to be able to turn themselves into dangerously attractive women.

### Grasshopper

Covering the general categories of locust and cricket, the grasshopper has a variety of meanings in different places. In ancient Greece, Athenians wore a golden grasshopper in their hair as an indication of their nobility. For Egyptians locusts were the deadly enemies of Maat, the goddess of cosmic order and provider of food and drink to her father, Re, the sun god. For Christians, when the baby Jesus holds a grasshopper it refers to the Egyptian plague of locusts and the subsequent conversion of pagans.

### Griffin

Also called griffon or gryphon. This mythical beast originated in the ancient East—Babylon, Persia, and Assyria—and has the head, wings, and claws of an eagle and the body of a lion; occasionally it is also given a serpent's tail. For Greeks and Romans the griffin was sacred to Minerva/Athena and is symbolic of sun and fire. In heraldry, griffins symbolize watchfulness and courage, and are often shown guarding gateways and entrances to important buildings.

### Horse

The horse was an important animal for ancient man, and has an important place in mythology. White horses were especially revered. The horse's importance is reflected in its position as a sun symbol: in many cultures, it draws the chariot of the sun god across the heavens to chase the powers of darkness from the heavens. The Celts worshiped a horse goddess named Epona who was a funeral deity; for them, the horse symbolized death and carried away the soul of the dead. A warrior was often buried with his horse, who represented courage, speed, and strength.

### Mermaid

This female siren with a fish tail is a medieval Christian symbol of lust and temptation; when she was shown holding a fish it was interpreted as a captured Christian soul. In folklore, however, mermaids were popularly supposed to make very good and fertile wives and were sought after. Their image was frequently used for decoration in folk objects.

### Monkey

In the Western world the monkey is always a symbol of wickedness—early Christians saw monkeys as the representation of the devil. A monkey carved on medieval buildings such as churches represented idle mischief. Later artists put an apple in the mouth of the monkey to represent the fall of man. In time the monkey came to represent the vanity of the man who indulged in luxury and indolence.

142

The owl has a long history as a symbol of wisdom; it was also the symbol of a true alchemist. It is, however, best known as the bird most sacred to Athena/Minerva, the Greco-Roman goddess of wisdom, and it is from this association that the owl has become an allegory for wisdom and ancient knowledge. Because the owl is nocturnal, it also represents sleep and occasionally night itself. Since ancient times the owl has been a bird of ill omen, foretelling death in many cultures from China to Britain, and it is often seen on funerary urns. For Native Americans and Maoris it is a nocturnal guardian against evil spirits.

### Peacock
The Romans believed that the peacock's flesh could not decay, so the bird was symbolic of immortality and was sacred to the goddess Juno. For early Christians, this was transposed into representing the resurrection of Christ, and the so-called eyes on its feathers came to symbolize foresight and prescience. In India, the peacock was seen as a royal bird and was used to support the throne of royalty, but it also symbolized love and beauty.

### Salamander
A type of lizard, the salamander was believed to live, eat, and breed within flames and was able to extinguish fire by walking on it. Christians adapted its image to represent enduring faith: with its nonflammable properties, the salamander could not be burned by the fires of temptation. It was used on baptismal fonts as a symbol of baptism by fire and water. A salamander was also used in late medieval times as a symbol of bravery and courage despite the flames of adversity.

Symbols from the Western Tradition

### Serpent

A creature found around the world, the serpent appears in many cultures and symbolizes many different things. For the Greeks and in many Asian cultures, the serpent symbolizes the force of evil. For Christians it symbolizes temptation and sin as told in the story of the Garden of Eden. In other cultures a serpent is a symbol of wisdom, as when it is shown twined around the Tree of Knowledge. A serpent biting its own tail represents eternity and is used around clock dials and on mourning jewelry.

### Swallow

This small bird has a place in Christian iconography as a symbol of the incarnation of Christ; it is often depicted in Nativity and Annunciation scenes. Furthermore, due to its annual spring migration from Africa it is also a symbol of the Resurrection. In China it is a symbol of spring, and it is considered lucky if the bird builds its nest under the eaves of your house for it will bring you happiness and good fortune. But in Japan the swallow symbolizes unfaithfulness because it is believed to change its mate frequently.

### Swan

In classical mythology the swan is supposed to sing just before it dies (hence the term "swan song")—this gives rise to its use as a symbol of a happy death. Swans pull Venus's chariot, so they are linked with love and the goddess herself, as well as with Apollo when he is the god of music. Because swans mate for life they are also a symbol of fidelity. In India, the Lord of Creation is often depicted flying on a swan as he travels from place to place. In Hindu mythology, swans symbolize sound judgment.

### Tortoise

Because of their long lifespan, tortoises symbolize longevity in many cultures. Ancient Greeks used the tortoise as a symbol of immortality. The Chinese believed that tortoises lived for a thousand years, so they too deemed tortoises symbolic of longevity. The Chinese also believed that the world rested on the back of a tortoise *(ao)* during creation. Similarly, the ancient Hindus believed that a giant tortoise holds up eight white elephants, which in turn support the world and the heavens.

### Unicorn

A fabulous beast occurring in ancient Persian and Egyptian mythology and a symbol of purity, the unicorn was adopted centuries later by Christians as a symbol of purity and chastity, particularly in connection with the Virgin Mary. In the early-fourteenth-century tradition of courtly love, the unicorn became the symbol of the smitten and deluded lover. Apothecaries used the unicorn in their trade signs, as the unicorn's horn was believed to be the antidote to all forms of poison.

### Winged horse

The ancient notion of a flying horse appears in many cultures. Perhaps the earliest known is from Etruscan tomb objects, where it is symbolic of the swift passage of life and an easy journey to the next world. This idea was adopted by early Christians, who used the motif of a winged horse in their catacombs. In Greek legend, the winged horse Pegasus stamped his hoof and broke the ground from which sprang the fountain of inspiration for the Muses.

### Wings

Wings are a symbol of divinity on a figure or an animal. They are also associated with speed, travel, and the passage of time, or they can be encircling, protective wings. Wings can indicate angels and saints, but many malign mythical beasts—harpy, griffin, wyvern—are winged to emphasize their power. Wings are of course derived from birds, and gods such as Horus assume a more awesome aspect thanks to their winged power. In Christian iconography a pair of white wings symbolizes the Holy Spirit.

### Wyvern

This mythical beast is a medieval symbol of war and pestilence. It has the body and head of a winged dragon plus a barbed tongue, a long, curling barbed serpent's tail, and two eagle's legs. This beast was probably concocted based on stories of exotic beasts brought back to Europe by travelers to the East. The wyvern is perhaps best known as the symbol of the principality of Wales in Great Britain.

### Anchor

Anchors are redolent of the seas and are used symbolically to infer all things maritime. A rope tangled around an anchor is typically found on sailors' tombs and symbolizes death. The anchor was an early Christian symbol of resilience against oppression and hope for the future. The anchor symbol has been found in the ancient catacombs of Rome, where early Christians buried their dead—there it was used as a substitute for the cross, since it contains the basic cross shape.

### Battle

This symbol of crossed swords is associated with death in battle. It is most commonly seen on maps to signify the site of a battle, often accompanied by the date of the encounter. The symbol of two crossed swords is also a synonym for military power and authority and has been used in that context on medals and badges. In genealogy the symbol is used as shorthand for "lost in battle" or "died in battle."

### Beard

The wearing of a beard is a symbol of wisdom, authority, and masculinity; it shows a man's strength and virility. In China, beards symbolize bravery and supernatural power as well as age and sagacity; venerable scholars and intellectuals sport long beards. In ancient Egypt, the gods wore long beards that curled at the ends while the pharaohs wore short beards. Greek sky gods such as Zeus wore beards, which symbolized falling rain or the sun's rays. Even some goddesses wore beards—for example, the Middle Eastern goddess Ishtar, in her form of Ashtoreth.

### Candle

Candlelight plays an important part in many religious rituals. For Christians it symbolizes Christ as the light of the world, bringing understanding and love to a dark universe. During Holy Week a candlestick with fifteen candles burns in front of the altar; one candle is extinguished each day until the last one is snuffed, which symbolizes the death of Christ. A burning candle also symbolizes the briefness of life and the way a light breeze (chance) can blow the flame out and death can come unexpectedly and early.

### Chains

Chains are associated with captivity and loss of freedom and are shown decorating old jails and houses of correction. During the Renaissance chains were used to symbolize man enslaved by his desires, thus all the Vices are shown fettered by chains. Because snakes in Christian teaching are inherently evil, chained serpents are symbolic of captive evil. However, gold chains signify the importance of office for local officials such as mayors.

### Cherub

Small winged infants are called cherubs, and in Christian iconography cherubim ("ones who pray") belong in the first hierarchy of angels and symbolize divine wisdom and innocence. Cherubim also occur in Jewish and Islamic cultures as God's throne bearers. In secular decoration they have been confused with, and are often interchangeable with, cupids. A cherub with crossed wings was used in Baroque times around the tombs of children.

### Comedy mask

This is nearly always seen together with the mask of tragedy, representing drama. The comedy mask wears a wide smile and is the attribute of Thalia, the muse of comedy and pastoral poetry. Both masks were popular devices of Greek drama used to indicate the type of character being played. The Romans also used masked players in their theaters—such masks were found on the walls of Pompeii.

### Tragedy mask

The symbol of drama always seen together with the mask of comedy. The tragedy mask wears a sad expression and is the attribute of Melpomene, the muse of tragedy. The masks allowed actors to play multiple roles and also magnified their voices to some extent. Both masks later were used decoratively along with musical instruments on printed advertisements and to indicate music halls and theaters.

### Crown

Crowns are an almost universal symbol of power and authority. An elaborate and expensive headdress is an ancient mark of honor and achievement. Crowns indicate royalty and authority—a crown literally puts its wearer above others by increasing his or her height and indicating with its magnificence their importance. It denotes possession of lands and peoples and is often seen on coats of arms both for individuals and municipal bodies. Greek gods and goddesses often wore a crown or circlet to indicate their divinity and authority.

### Cymbals

The cymbal is one of the oldest musical instruments, and two cymbals symbolize the northern and southern hemispheres. They are associated particularly with the ancient Greek cult of Attis. An initiate to the cult drank from a cymbal and ate from a tambourine. The cult was served by a eunuch priesthood (the Galloi) in honor and recognition of Attis's self-castration, and then they slashed their arms in frenzy during their ecstatic dancing as a sign of mourning. Elsewhere the followers of Dionysus/Bacchus made drunken, cacophonous music with cymbals, drum, and tambourine during their orgies.

### Fasces

This bound bundle of (originally) birch rods also often enclosing an ax head was the symbol of authority of ancient Roman magistrates. The rods show the magistrates' power to have offenders flogged and the ax symbolizes their authority to have serious offenders beheaded. The fasces were used decoratively for many centuries before being adopted by the Italian fascist movement in Italy in the 1930s and 1940s. The fasces were also used by Cardinal Mazarin (1602–1661) as his badge; he had them carved on the doors of the Palais de L'Institut in Paris.

### Feather

Those who wear feathers are associated with the soaring powers of birds and in particular with the merciless hunter-killer birds of prey. Feathers symbolize truth, lightness, speed, and flight. Two feathers together symbolize the elements of light and air. A white feather represents clouds but also cowardice (from the belief that a cock with a white tail feather is poorly bred and not good for cockfighting).

### Fire

Fire symbolizes destruction but also divine energy and is another universal symbol of the power of the gods. A ball of flame is the manifestation of the appearance of a god on earth in many cultures and religions. For ancient Egyptians fire was purifying. In ancient Iran fire was the personification of Atar, who protected the world against evil and guarded the chariot of the sun; his Aryan followers developed a fire cult devoted to him. In China fire. is a positive force meaning elemental drives such as awareness of danger, lust, and wrath. For Christians fire is a manifestation of the Holy Ghost and is important for purification; it also represents the threat of the fires of hell.

### Fleur-de-lis

The fleur-de-lis is a three-petal stylized flower, originally supposed to be either a lily or an iris. It is a symbol of purity and in Christian iconography is used to symbolize the Virgin Mary. In A.D. 493 the Merovingian king Clovis adopted the fleur-de-lis to show his purity and spirituality when he converted to Christianity. It has been widely used in church decoration since early times. From the twelfth century it has been used in the French royal arms, and it is also the emblem of the Italian city of Florence and of the powerful Farnese family.

### Grail

In Western tradition the grail represents the cosmic center or the cup of wisdom that contains the waters of life. It is described as a chalice that contains everything a man desires and was the legendary quest for King Arthur's Knights of the Round Table. It was supposed to grant immortality to those who drank from it. In Christian teaching the grail is Jesus' cup from the Last Supper and the cup in which Joseph of Aramathea collected Jesus' blood while he was nailed to the cross.

### Harp

As one of the earliest instruments, the harp is often used as a symbol of divine music and is seen in the arms of angels and mystical beings. The ancient Egyptians used a three-stringed harp that was symbolic of their three seasons—drought, deluge, and growth. The harp is associated with Terpsichore, the muse of dance and song. An early Irish king named David used a harp as his device and it consequently became symbolic of Ireland itself.

### Heart

This ultimate symbol of love is widely used around the world. It signifies not just pure love but also profane love. A flaming heart is symbolic of burning ardor. The heart is a popular symbol of fidelity and is often used in folk crafts, particularly in the work of central and northern European craftsmen. They took this favorite motif with them to America where it is especially seen in Pennsylvania Dutch works.

### Helmet

The significance of helmets lies in their association with war as an essential piece of armor. However, the helmet is also an attribute of the Roman goddess Minerva, the patron of wisdom learning, civilization, and benevolence. So helmets are often shown on old buildings of learning, such as libraries and schools. The virtues of faith and fortitude in human form are shown wearing helmets as a symbol of protection and preservation.

### Horn of plenty/cornucopia

The horn of plenty—a goat's horn spilling fruit and ears of wheat—is a classical symbol of abundance, affluence, and fertility across many cultures. It derives from the Greek legend that tells how the baby Zeus was suckled by a goat and later gave the goat thanks by breaking off its horn and declaring that its owner would always have good things in abundance. Known as the Horn of Amalthea to Hellenic cultures, it also came to symbolize peace and became a popular symbol in commerce. It is also known as the Cornucopia, and is an ancient and powerful symbol said to attract all kinds of wealth and luck.

### Horseshoe

Today the horseshoe is one of the most commonly seen symbols of good luck, especially when it is given to newlyweds. The horseshoe first was used as a symbol of protection in the Middle Ages when it was hung over the entrance or doorway. This may be a remnant of early Celtic horse-worshipping cults. To bring good luck, a horseshoe must be placed with the ends turned up so that the luck can't fall out.

### Hourglass

An hourglass contains the sands of time and is symbolic of time passing and life running out. In particular, an hourglass symbolizes the transitory nature of life and indicates that death is unavoidable. Death and Old Father Time invariably carry an hourglass to remind mankind of the passage of time. Hourglasses were a popular motif on tombs and memorials in the eighteenth century.

### Knot

The knot is an obvious symbol of unity and fidelity and of two people joined together in marriage into one unified whole. The Celts used intricate knotwork decoration on most of their important objects, and these elaborate patterns seem to have no beginning and no end and were, perhaps, symbolic of the neverending circle of life and death repeating itself for eternity. The ancient Egyptians believed that knots held magic power, and they associated knots with binding and releasing. They revered the knot as the symbol of the hidden force of germination in the Aser tree that brought out the sun god Re every day.

### Scythe

One of the attributes of Father Time, especially in his persona as the Reaper. The scythe symbolizes time cut short or a life cut off. Death, when shown as a skeleton, often carries a scythe. The scythe is also an attribute of Saturn, the Roman god of agriculture. Later Saturn merged with Cronus, the Greek god of time, who then merged into Father Time and then Death, the Grim Reaper. For Christians a scythe is carried by the Angel of Death who uses it to "harvest" the souls of mortals.

### Sickle

This ancient agricultural tool is a universal symbol of harvest and plenty and is often shown cutting a sheaf of wheat. It is an attribute of Demeter, the Greek goddess of animal husbandry and good harvest, and also of Priapus, the rustic god of orchards, fields, and flocks. The personification of summer as one of the Four Seasons also carries a sickle. The sickle was used as one of the emblems of the Soviet Union, for whom it represented agriculture.

### Skull

Many Tibetan and Hindu deities use a human skull as an ornament, as the head of a club, or as a container for blood. Shiva wears a human skull and often a necklace made of skulls to symbolize his role as the destroyer and bringer of death. In the West, the skull is symbolic of mortality and the quick passing of life as well as worldly vanity. It first really started to appear in Europe in the fifteenth century, when it was used to decorate tombs and cemeteries. It is often used as a macabre decoration around funerary objects.

### Skull and crossbones

Popularly assumed by pirates as their emblem, the skull and crossbones indicates almost certain death and at the very least deadly danger. The skull is symbolic of the vital life force contained in the head and the crossbones are thigh bones, indicative of the vital force contained in the loins. It is often seen on tombstones as a commemorative decoration. The symbol is widely used to indicate toxic liquids and fumes, and life-threatening situations.

### Sunburst

Also called the sun-in-glory and sun-in splendor, this symbolizes illumination and understanding in many cultures, as well as the source of life itself. The rayed sun symbolizes the center of the universe and the heart of understanding and intelligence. For Christians the sunburst often accompanies a dove, which is symbolic of the Holy Spirit.

### Terrestrial globe

This symbol of exploration and navigation came into being only after the repudiation of the flat earth theory in the Renaissance. Then it was taken up as a general symbol of scientific endeavor; it became an attribute of Astronomy and Geometry and was used on the façades of important buildings. When the personifications of justice and fame carry a globe, it symbolizes universality, as it does when used in a Christian context, meaning the spread of Christianity across the globe.

### Urn

An urn is used as a container for the ashes of the dead, so it is traditionally a symbol of loss and mourning dating from classical times, when it began to be used on funerary monuments. An empty urn represents mourning and death and consequently symbolizes loss. Closed urns allude to the containment of the ashes of the dead. Sometimes a flame issues from the top to symbolize resurrection. The Mesopotamian goddess Ishtar carries an urn containing the waters of life, symbolizing fertility.

### Wheel

The wheel appears in many guises in many cultures. It is symbolic of the passage of time and the transience of fortune as the Wheel of Fortune, and represents Tyche, the goddess of chance and changing fortune. It also symbolizes the sun. In Christian iconography the wheel is an attribute of St. Catherine, who was martyred on a wheel; legend lives on at English bonfires in the form of a firework known as a Catherine wheel. Wheels also symbolize speed and were a popular motif on early railroad stations.

### Windmill

The sails of a moving windmill that are turning without grinding symbolize sloth and the passage of time. Windmills turn with the direction of the wind and symbolize man's fickle nature. For Christians the windmill signifies heavenly bread made by man that has been ground by the stones of derision, powered by the winds of fury. In European allegory, to tilt at a windmill, like Don Quixote, is a sure sign of madness.

### Acorn

The seed of the mighty oak was used in Celtic and Scandinavian art to symbolize fecundity, life, and immortality. It also symbolized the oak tree itself. The Romans also used the acorn as a motif. The acorn in later times became symbolic of growth and it is seen on banks and commercial buildings in allusion to the proverb "Great oaks from little acorns grow."

### Anemone

The brilliantly colored anemone originates from Asia Minor, where it is an ancient symbol of death and mourning. The Greek *animos* means "wind," an allusion to its beauty being as welcome as a light wind and as brief. In English its common name is "wind flower." In Greek mythology, anemones sprouted from the spilled blood of Adonis. In a parallel medieval myth, anemones are said to have grown on Calvary where Christ's blood fell on the ground.

### Apple

The apple is a fruit of wet northern climates and in many cultures symbolizes immortality. For the Celts it represented mythical Avalon, the Island of Apples, but it was also the fruit of the underworld. Norse myths speak of the golden apples of immortality, as do Greek myths, in which the golden apples of the Hesperides were a wedding gift from Gaia to Zeus and Hera. The apple is important in Christian symbolism as the fruit of temptation growing on the Tree of Knowledge that caused Eve and Adam to be expelled from the Garden of Eden. In Christian iconography, the baby Jesus holding an apple symbolizes the doctrine of Redemption.

### Bay tree

Also called laurel, this is a highly aromatic evergreen tree originating in the Mediterranean area. The ancient Greeks and Romans used bay as a strong symbol of resurrection and renewal, glory and honor, and sacred to the god Apollo. They adorned their heroes—poets, soldiers, athletes—with crowns made of bay. As a long-lived evergreen, the bay also symbolizes eternity and was used on monuments and memorials to indicate that the deed or person would never be forgotten. In ancient times, bay trees were planted near buildings to protect them from lightning.

### Birch tree

According to Viking legend, the last battle in the world will be fought around a birch tree. The birch is sacred to the gods Thor, Donar, and Frigga. The birch symbolizes light and fertility, and protects against the work of witches and evil spirits, hence the use of birch swatches to beat felons and lunatics. The cosmic tree or sky ladder of shamanism is a birch: the shaman is required to climb up seven or nine notches to symbolize his ascent through the layers of the planetary spheres to reach the Supreme Spirit.

### Carnation

Old-fashioned carnations possessed a strong, spicy scent, and in China this led to the carnation being one of the Five Senses and an attribute of the personification of Smell. It was a Chinese symbol of marriage. For Christians red carnations symbolize the blood of martyrs, while the white carnation symbolizes virginal purity. Carnations were said to grow where the Virgin Mary's tears fell on the road to Calvary. In Renaissance art carnations were used as a symbol of betrothal.

### Egg

Eggs are important symbolically in many cultures: they symbolize the germ of creation, the cosmic womb, and beginnings. The "cosmic egg" is at the heart of the creation myths of the Chinese, Greek, Egyptian, Phoenician, Japanese, Indian, Pacific Island, Central American, and Norse stories. The Egyptian Book of the Dead says that the first god emerged from an egg that had lain hidden in a marsh. The Chinese creation myth says the Cosmic Egg broke open and the yolk became the sky and the albumen the earth. For Buddhists the eggshell is the "shell of ignorance" broken asunder during second birth.

### Fig

The species *Ficus carica* is the fig tree familiar to Europeans, in which the ancient Greeks saw explicit erotic symbolism. They saw the fruit of the fig as a phallic shape, and when it was cut open it became the vulva. Consequently it was sacred to Venus, the goddess of love, and to Dionysus, the god of wine and erotic pleasure. For Jews and later Christians, the fig was the Tree of Knowledge whose fruit Eve ate in the Garden of Eden. It symbolized lust, desire, and "forbidden fruits" and provided the leaves for Adam and Eve to cover their nakedness.

### Grapevine

Grapevines are a symbol of harvest and the season of fall. The fruits are also used as a symbol of fertility. Grapevines are significant in Jewish culture and can often be found as decorative features in synagogues, with the twelve bunches of grapes symbolizing the twelve tribes of Israel. For early Christians the vine symbolized Christ, the branches his disciples, and the grapes the blood/wine of Christ. Grapes are sacred to the Greek Dionysus (Roman Bacchus), the god of wine, and symbolize revelry, drunkenness, and excess.

### Hawthorn

Common in European hedgerows, the hawthorn was revered as a fairy tree that possesses the power to ward off evil and protect against sorcery. A hawthorn tree was believed to be the meeting place for spirits and fairies. When a young girl wears a white hawthorn blossom circlet it symbolizes her purity from evil and her virginity. Hawthorn blossom was used as a bridal flower in Greece and Rome and was sacred to Hecate, the goddess of the moon, magic, and enchantment; Flora, the goddess of fruitfulness and flowers; and Maia, the goddess of fertility.

### Hazel

Hazelnuts are associated with the Mother Goddess and are a symbol of hidden wisdom. They also symbolize peace and lovers. The hazel is a magical tree and is credited with being a rainmaker; hazel wands can divine water in the right hands. In Norse and Teutonic mythology, the hazel was sacred to Thor, the irascible god of the weather. In ancient Greece, the staff of Hermes, the messenger of the gods, was made of hazel — a symbol of communication and reconciliation.

### Holly

Now synonymous with Western Christmas celebrations, the holly has an ancient pedigree as a sacred tree. It was important for Saturn, the Roman god of agriculture, workers, and vine growers. His festival of Saturnalia (December 17–23) was a time of feasting and merriment when everything, even conflict, stopped. It was the only time of year when it was not unlucky to bring holly boughs into the home. The Druids believed that the holly was sacred and kept lightning at bay, and they considered it unlucky to cut down a holly.

### Ivy

Because of the way that ivy grows by clinging tightly to whatever it encounters, it has become a symbol of friendship, fidelity, and marriage. As an evergreen plant, it is also symbolic of immortality and eternal life. Ivy is sacred to the gods Dionysus and Bacchus, the Greek and Roman deities of fertility, revelry, and drinking. The ancient Greeks valued and used ivy for its narcotic and medicinal properties, and consequently it became an attribute of lyric poetry. The Celts used ivy and holly for their midwinter festival to celebrate the warrior deity Brân.

### Lily

Due to its heavenly scent and perfect beauty, the white Madonna lily is an ancient symbol of purity that was associated with Hera, the wife of Zeus, and all matters feminine such as marriage, fertility, and childbirth. The lily symbolizes her mother's milk. Christian iconography has made this lily a symbol of the Virgin Mary (hence the name), and she is often shown holding them. White lilies are also used in funerary decoration as symbols of piety and innocence, particularly associated with children and young women.

### Mistletoe

The mistletoe (*Viscum album*) is an evergreen parasitic plant found on apple trees, hawthorns, and oaks among others. In Europe it is a symbol of life and a powerful protective talisman as well as a healing plant. Mistletoe was sacred to the Druids, who supposedly cut it with a golden sickle on the sixth day of the moon when it was needed for a ritual sacrifice of two white bulls. Ancient Britons believed that it ensured the continued life of the tree spirit through the dark, cold days of winter.

### Olive

This ancient Mediterranean tree can live for hundreds, sometimes thousands, of years. The evergreen olive tree symbolizes immortality, fruitfulness, and plenty. The olive tree is sacred to the goddess Athena/Minerva and the god Zeus/Jupiter in recognition of its universal usefulness as a source of nutrition and medication as well as all the myriad applications for olive oil. At the ancient Olympic games, a crown of olive leaves was given to the best athlete to signify his achievement. The Romans in particular used olive wreaths to symbolize victory, peace, and wealth.

### Pineapple

In ancient times the pineapple was a popular symbol of fertility, especially in the Middle East where it grew readily. It was rarely seen in Europe until the seventeenth century, when the first pineapples started to appear on the tables of the wealthy. At this time, this highly decorative fruit became a symbol of hospitality and wealth and was consequently a popular decorative feature on gateposts and at entrances of grand houses.

### Poppy

This beautiful plant has been known since ancient times as an opiate for medicinal use, a painkiller, and a recreational drug. The Greeks revered it as an attribute of Hypnos, the god of sleep, and his son Morpheus, the god of dreams. In classical funerary art the poppy symbolized the sleep of death. After World War I, when the killing fields of northern France exploded with delicate red poppies, the flower came to symbolize the thousands of soldiers who died there. The poppy is used to this day during annual remembrance festivals.

### Rose

In ancient times, the rose symbolized beauty, purity, and fertility across many cultures. A rose garden for the Romans was a symbol of paradise and was a popular motif on tombs in the Roman catacombs. It is also symbolic of paradise in Islamic belief. For Christians the rose is an attribute of the Virgin Mary (the flower shows her purity and the thorns her suffering); the red rose symbolizes martyrdom and the white piety. However, since Renaissance times the rose has also become a symbol of secrecy.

### Sunflower

The brilliant yellow sunflower has been a popular motif since the seventeenth century, when the plant was introduced into Europe from the New World. It symbolizes constancy, devotion to the point of infatuation, and particularly remembrance. It also symbolizes the undying love of God, because of the way the sunflower follows the path of the sun over the course of the day, constantly turning to keep its face in the brightest light. Alternatively, its slavish devotion to the sun symbolizes unreliability and false riches. For the Chinese the sunflower possesses magical powers and is symbolic of longevity.

### Tree of Life

In the creation myths of the Assyrians, Persians, Indians, and a number of other ancient Asian and Middle Eastern cultures, this tree was the source of life itself. The tree lives on the flat earth with its deep roots growing far down into the ground, its branches reaching high into the sky and supporting the heavens. The tree is variously a date palm, a fig, a sycamore, an olive, or a grape vine. The Romans and Greeks also had myths about the Tree of Life, which for them was an oak with its leaves and branches in the heavens and its root in the underworld.

### Weeping willow

In ancient Egypt, the willow was sacred to the god Osiris, the ruler of the netherworld. The willow tree sheltered his coffin while his soul turned into a phoenix, which then sat in the tree. The willow therefore symbolized the resurrection of the god. In the West, the graceful willow appears bent down with sorrow and has long symbolized mourning and sadness and has been extensively used in funerary art on monuments and mourning cards. In the seventeenth century, the willow became associated with grief; forsaken lovers and rejected suitors would wear a wreath or hat of willow.

### Wheat

As an essential food source, the wheat sheaf or single ear of wheat has been used as an important symbol of fecundity and fertility in virtually all farming cultures. Ceres and Demeter, the goddesses of agriculture of Rome and Greece, both have wheat as one of their attributes. Wheat is also symbolic of summer in many cultures. In Christian iconography a wheat sheaf is often presented alongside a bunch of grapes to represent the Eucharist, with the wheat symbolizing the body and the grape the blood of Christ.

### Wreath

The ancient Greeks and Romans wove sweet bay (often called laurel), oak, or olive leaves into circlets with which to crown their heroes. Such wreaths were used to honor emperors, poets, musicians, athletes, soldiers, and heroes of all descriptions. The wreath symbolized sovereignty and glory, honor and victory, and was only awarded to a worthy recipient. More recently funeral wreaths composed of flowers symbolize death and sorrow at parting and remembrance.

# American Symbols

Symbolism has been used extensively by the indigenous people of North America for thousands of years, with designs placed on all manner of domestic objects, as well as in more permanent places such as totem poles. Some of the oldest symbolic images are on rock faces, where they are known as petroglyphs. The arts and crafts of Native Americans are rarely without decoration, with symbols of animals and geometric patterns being particularly popular.

The term "Native Americans" covers peoples from a vast geographical area, and a symbol may have a particular meaning in one area and a completely different meaning in another. It is also important to note that many of the symbols have been interpreted by modern-day Anglo-Europeans and may have meanings different from those originally intended.

Every century, as the need arises, new symbols are created for a specific purpose. During the 1930s a whole language of signs was developed by and for a particular group of people. A few hobos, or migratory workers, still travel the roads and railroads of North America, but their heyday was the Great Depression, when tens of thousands of people lost their homes and took to traveling in search of work. The work was often temporary, seasonal, and low-paid; many worked in the fields picking and packing fruit and vegetables.

As the different harvest times of various crops came and went, migrant workers would travel to find their next job. Their mode of transport was inevitably as illegal passengers in railroad boxcars. In order to make their harsh lives a little easier, a communication system was created using basic symbols. These would be drawn—usually in chalk or coal—on fences, trees, or other suitable positions to inform or warn fellow travelers as to what was ahead. Some of the symbols are easily interpreted, others are deliberately obscure.

### Abundance

The symbol of a large mountain or mountain range is used to represent abundance for two main reasons: First, the shape of a mountain can mean a "large heap" in many cultures, and so would be used in times of plenty to refer to things like the products of good harvests. Second, mountainous regions are often full of game animals, fruit, berries, and other natural products that would signify a state of abundance.

### Alertness

The arrowhead is used to symbolize alertness. When a hunter or warrior was relaxed, he would carry his arrows in a quiver on his back or his side, but when he spotted prey or danger, he would drop to the ground and draw an arrow from the quiver. It would then be "nocked," that is, placed in position on the bow with the arrowhead facing the target, and he would be ready for action.

### Bright prospects

The symbol of thunderbird tracks means "bright prospects." When animal tracks are depicted in Native American images, they symbolize the presence of that animal rather than the animal itself—that is, the idea that the animal has been here, or will be here. This symbol signifies that the thunderbird will come, bringing rain with him and ending the dry season, and there will be good crops and plenty for all.

## Captivity

A lasso is a length of rope with a noose at one end. The lasso is whirled around and at the critical moment released in the direction of the object for capture, flying through the air to land, hopefully, on its target—usually the head and neck of an animal. It is then pulled taut, and the animal brought to the ground or tied up. It is not surprising therefore, that the symbol of the lasso is used to indicate captivity.

## Chief

A tribal chief is usually represented by eagle feathers; this is because the eagle is seen as a divine spirit, chief of the animal world, and a close associate of the sun gods. The eagle is also seen as a protector against evil spirits, hence the analogy in the symbolism of the chief. Feathers are used to represent creativity or a person of honor, and are used in prayers.

## Coyote tracks

The tracks of coyotes or wolves generally indicate a direction. Being social animals that often have to travel long distances through dense undergrowth or snow, they usually move nose to tail. This is seen as a significant parallel to how people move in such circumstances, and since the animals are also symbols of leadership, their tracks are seen as strong markers of pathways through forests and other remote places.

### Defiance

The snake symbolizes defiance or wisdom. It is also often found in healing and fertility rites due to its universal connection with masculinity. Where this symbol is used, it is usually depicted with its forked tongue extended, and is often associated with the speed of lightning. Its ability to move undetected and its reputation as a hunter made this a popular but powerful symbol in many tribal areas throughout America.

### Enclosure for ceremonial dance

For thousands of years, an important part of Native American tribal life has been ritual ceremony, and an integral part of such events is often the ceremonial dance. Ceremonial dances can take many forms, from enacting the myths and legends of the tribe to communing with the spirits to ask for good weather, plentiful crops, or good luck in hunting or warfare. The places where the dances take place are of great significance, and are often situated within man-made structures—as depicted by the symbol.

### Everlasting life

The butterfly has many different meanings throughout the Indian nations, but a common theme is "immortality." This is probably due in a large part to the American monarch butterflies that every year migrate thousands of miles from Mexico and California north to Canada, and then return to congregate in countless millions. The cyclic rebirth of butterflies through metamorphosis is also a powerful symbol used extensively throughout the Americas.

### Four ages of man

The passage of time is important in any culture linked to the land, due to the changing seasons and the repeating patterns of life, death, and rebirth. This is symbolized by the sign for the four ages of man, which is circular, indicating that there is no start or finish to life. This endless cyclic process is fundamental to the cultures of many Native Americans, and so makes this an important symbol.

### Friendship

Arrows are a powerful symbol to any warrior race for several reasons: not only do they indicate the ability and willingness to fight, but since they are usually made by the archer who will use them, they are highly personal artifacts. Arrows nearly always carry the markings of the owner—a well-made arrow represents a lot of hard work, especially if it has a flint or metal head. The symbol of two crossed arrows therefore can be used to indicate friendship between two people or tribes.

### Good omen

The sign of bear tracks is generally intended as a good omen wherever it is displayed. The paws of a bear are considered to be a link to the spirit world of the animal, or to indicate that the bear's spirit is already present. This symbol is also associated with badger paws, which hold great significance due to the reverence in which badgers are held as healers and persistent hunters (their tracks indicate good health and great strength). Both bear and badger tracks also denote leadership.

### Good prospects

The symbol for "good prospects" is similar to that for "bright prospects," except that this one is more direct. Both are linked to the arrival of rain, which is vital to every agricultural economy, but where the thunderbird symbol means "rain is expected," the cloud symbol means "rain is here," and so people could be confident that the crops were going to thrive and they could look forward to good times.

### Guarding

The sign of a fence is used to denote "guarding good luck," because a tribe's prosperity is directly related to the abundance of its harvests or the number of livestock kept. Farming communities build fences to keep crops safe from animals such as deer and rabbits, and also to keep their livestock from wandering off and getting lost or eaten by wolves, coyotes, or mountain lions. The symbol of the fence therefore represents looking after one's good luck.

### Guidance

In early morning, the planet Venus is the brightest object in the sky until the sun rises. It is known as the "morning star," and has been an important symbol to human cultures since civilization began, although it has been interpreted differently over many thousands of years. To the Native Americans it is usually seen as an important spirit, indicating purity and courage. It is the symbol of spirit guidance.

### Horse

The horse is a relative newcomer to the Americas, since it was introduced by Spanish invaders just four hundred years ago. Nevertheless, the horse quickly became an extremely important part of Native American life, and soon came to symbolize strength, power, endurance, loyalty, and mobility. The arrival of horses meant that for the first time hunters could chase large bison herds for long distances, and as a result a time of plenty came to many native populations.

### Journey

The symbol for a journey is depicted by a pair of saddlebags. This is because when long journeys are undertaken, there is often little time for hunting or gathering supplies, and so food and other essential items have to be carried—usually in saddlebags slung over the backs of horses. The distances traveled on horseback, especially by the Plains Indians, were often vast. As a result, there was a direct association between carrying supplies and traveling.

### Leading to happiness

Many native cultures make direct associations between weather phenomena or observations of celestial bodies and current or future events. A sky band is used in images to symbolize "the way that leads to happiness," and is often shown above a god, king, or tribal chief. It may also be shown along with symbols for the sun, clouds, stars, or constellations.

 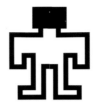 

### Lighthearted

The bird is a popular symbol for Native Americans, with different species representing different things. The bird is perceived to be free of the constraints of normal life: it is able to fly up and away wherever and whenever it chooses. Small birds also sing their joy out to the world and are therefore seen as carefree. This combination of freedom and happiness makes an excellent sign for lightheartedness.

### Man

The symbol for man is, unsurprisingly, one of the oldest used by humans in representations of their activities. Some take the form of carvings in bone, ivory, or stone, whereas others are simple paintings in caves or on rock faces. In these, the images of men were often involved in scenes depicting successful hunting parties or victorious warriors. Over the years, many different designs have been used to denote "man" or "men," but they tend to be very similar in concept throughout the Americas.

### Paths crossing

Paths crossing are simply represented by the sign of a cross—this is a significant symbol because in sparsely populated areas, places where paths or tracks cross are important meeting places. Indeed, many settlements originated at crossroads for this reason: people would gather at such locations for many purposes, including trade, tribal discussions, and ritual celebrations. Where trading was particularly profitable, these sites often became permanent.

### Peace

For Native Americans, one of the main purposes of symbolic images is to convey the current status of a tribe or village. The primary message would be whether the local people were prosperous and healthy, and whether they were at war with another tribe or in a state of peace. Since a declaration of peace was often ritualized by the ceremonial breaking of an arrow, the symbol of a broken arrow was a natural choice to denote peace.

### Plentiful crops

Many of the traditional lands of the Native Americans are arid places, where rain is vital to the growth of crops, good harvests, and the prosperity of the people. In these areas, rain is seen as a blessing, and the sign of raindrops or rain clouds is used to denote plentiful crops. These symbols are also used to indicate the passing of the seasons, and thus denote change, fertility, and rebirth.

### Plenty game

The sign of deer tracks means that plenty of game animals may be found in the area; as such, this is a symbol of prosperity. Since deer provide meat, skin, antler horn, sinew, and many other important by-products, their presence also means safety and shelter. Sinew is used in the manufacture of hunting bows, arrows, and other important implements. Deerskin was used to make shoes, clothes, tents, and many vital domestic items.

### Protection

The arrow is such an important part of any culture that relies on the bow for hunting and defense that it is the obvious symbol to represent protection. The direction of the arrow is often also of significance; if it is pointing right it can mean protection against physical enemies, and if it is pointing left it can mean defending against evil spirits.

### Sign of the desert

A large part of North America is covered by deserts, so there are many different symbols for such places. Two of the most common are the cactus and the Gila monster. The connection between arid lands and the cactus is obvious, even to those who have never seen a desert. Until recently, knowledge of local plants and animals was fundamental for Native Americans, and the Gila monster—which only lives in hot, dry places— was often used to represent the desert.

### Strength

The rattlesnake was, and still is, revered by Native Americans as a symbol of great power. The strength of the snake's poison is legendary, and the way a rattlesnake strikes—the action of lunging forward and biting its prey—is very powerful symbolically. The sign of a rattlesnake jaw is used to differentiate it from the usual snake symbol, and where it is incorporated into images it indicates great strength.

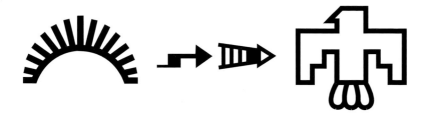

### Sun symbol

The sun has been worshiped by many human cultures, but more or less all of them have regarded the sun as a symbol of all that is good: warmth, prosperity, and above all, happiness. There are many different forms of the sun symbol — some are very stylized, whereas others are simple designs. To some extent this is dictated by the medium on which they are being shown; in basket weaving, for instance, they may be woven into the structure, and therefore need to be inherently simple shapes.

### Swiftness

Lightning has been used by many cultures, including Native American peoples, to indicate speed, and many different lightning symbols have been used for this purpose. The speed of arrows is often linked to this symbolism with the depiction of the "lightning arrow." The innate power of thunder and lightning has been tied into the interpretation of spirit forces for many thousands of years, so these symbols have great significance.

### Thunderbird

The thunderbird is one of the few symbols used throughout the Native American nations, where it universally means "bearer of happiness" or "sacred bearer of happiness unlimited." It is used extensively on many arts and crafts, especially on jewelry. The thunderbird was a giant mythical bird that brought thunder by clapping his wings. His representatives were clowns who displayed wisdom through foolish acts, and he therefore brought happiness both through laughter and by heralding the arrival of rain.

### Universal brotherhood

For the Hopi, universal brotherhood is an ideal state in which there is no conflict. The Hopi have lived in the same area of northeastern Arizona for over 1,600 years. In this harsh arid environment, they cultivate corn, beans, and squash, and to bring rain for their crops they perform the Snake Dance. Their social structure contains a number of interlocking social and religious organizations with annual ceremonies punctuating the calendar. They never accepted Christianity despite many attempts by missionaries, and after 1780 they were left alone to follow their indigenous culture.

### Warding off evil spirits

The spirit world is of great importance to all Native American peoples, and various spirits are considered to be either good or evil. Good spirits include the thunderbird, which brings plenty, and the butterfly, which indicates everlasting life. Evil spirits include those that bring bad things like disease, drought, or poverty. The symbol for "warding off evil" is designated by two arrows pointing at a black circle that represents a generalized evil spirit— effectively warning that evil is not welcome.

### Wise/watchful

The medicine man was an important and revered member of any tribe. He conducted many religious or ritualistic acts, such as burial ceremonies and offerings to the spirits. The medicine man would also supply the tribe with remedies and potions for all manner of purposes, including those to ward off evil and for healing sickness or injury. Since he was synonymous with wisdom, the sign of the medicine man's eye means wise or watchful.

### Alcohol town
The sign for alcohol being available in a town dates back to the 1920s and early 1930s, the era of Prohibition, when alcoholic beverages were banned. This was a law known as the "Noble Experiment," which was passed in an attempt to reduce crime and corruption and solve social problems. It failed miserably, but there are still areas that frown on the sale and use of alcohol.

### Armed and hostile man
This sign indicates not only that the man living here is armed but also that he is likely to shoot if given any reason to do so. Most hobos would take this as a sign to pass by, but if it is necessary to approach the house, one would try to find a way to do so without risking antagonizing the owner.

### Beware—crime scene
This sign is very similar to that for a prison, except that the vertical lines are tilted over, and it has only two horizontal lines. The link with criminals being present is clear and is a good warning that everyone, including hobos, should keep out of the area. This is not just to avoid becoming the victim of another crime—it is to avoid being used as a scapegoat.

**American Symbols**

177

### Beware of thieves

Even though hobos rarely have much to steal, knowing that there are thieves about is important, mainly because the first person to be blamed for a theft is going to be the nearest hobo, even though he may be entirely innocent. Since word of thieves spreads quickly in a community, keeping a low profile at such times is always a good idea, especially if local vigilantes or overzealous police officers might make an appearance.

### Caution—judge lives here

As far as hobos are concerned, the presence of a judge can be good or bad, depending on the judge's attitude and the circumstances. A judge can be bad news if you are receiving sentence for an offense, but he may also represent the only chance for justice if local law enforcement officers have been overly aggressive.

### Courthouse in town

The sign for a courthouse may be displayed at a town's limits, near the official nameplate. Usually a hobo would not want to go near a courthouse, but there are occasions when a courthouse is important: official papers may have to be witnessed or processed by judges, especially in remote areas. These include the paperwork for registering marriages and births and for completing death certificates.

### Danger!

The three things that a traveling hobo needs every day are sustenance, shelter, and safety. The sign of three parallel lines means "danger," a symbol that most hobos would heed and pass through the area as quickly as possible. The biggest threat to safety would be from aggressive locals.

### Danger—be alert

When a hobo approaches an unknown town it is impossible for him to tell whether it is a safe place. Often the realization that a location is dangerous comes when it is too late, and so this warning sign can help a hobo decide whether to pass through or around such a place, and whether it is a good idea to carry a defensive weapon.

### Danger—don't drink the water

The most important thing a traveling hobo needs is clean water—while food is important, an adequate intake of liquid is more so. The problem is that on the road it can be difficult or impossible to tell if a source of water is fit to drink until it is too late. Seemingly good water can be contaminated by substances from deep underground, like arsenic, which can make anyone who consumes it very ill—it can even kill them.

### Dangerous dog lives here

Aggressive animals are just one kind of threat in the daily life of a hobo, and knowing that a vicious dog lives at a particular house can be lifesaving. Some owners would be only too happy to see a hobo get attacked and driven off by their canine guardian; others are not so unfriendly and will call off their dogs to allow a hobo to approach. Dog bites can cause severe injuries, and since medical treatment generally costs money, most hobos would want to steer clear of vicious pets.

### Free food

When a location has been identified as being good for a handout, the sign of a circle with a cross within it is made. The circle refers to the place and the cross means "OK." This may be a private house or the back door of a restaurant or rest stop where sympathetic staff give hungry hobos leftovers from their customers' meals.

### Free handouts to go

Although hobos are not necessarily disliked by people, they are also not universally liked. Some folk are not overtly rude but will often provide free handouts just so a hobo will go away. This sign is therefore useful when times are hard and an easy meal is needed.

### Free medical help

As if the struggle to find food, clean water, and safe shelter were not enough, the rigors of life on the road are likely to lead to eventual sickness or injury. Getting medical attention when it is needed is considered a luxury beyond the means of most hobos, so when a doctor is found who doesn't charge the needy, this symbol is displayed to let fellow travelers know.

### Free phone call

There are many reasons why a hobo might want to know where there is a free telephone: if he or she is looking for work, for instance, it is always a good idea to call ahead to see if any employment is available. Most hobos have family or friends somewhere, and even though they have chosen to go on the road, it doesn't mean they don't want to keep in touch with their loved ones.

### Go the other way

Crossroads and junctions are favorite locations for displaying hobo signs; this way a traveler can make an informed decision about which road to take. This sign can clearly save a lot of time and effort. It may mean that the locals are unfriendly or simply that the road is a dead end due to snow, floods, mountains, or desert.

### Good campsite

Most people take for granted having a secure place to sleep; hobos, however, have to deal with this every night. There are many risks, and physical violence from aggressive locals is one major problem, especially if they have consumed large quantities of alcohol. A sign indicating that a landowner is not going to cause problems if a hobo camps there is a very useful piece of information.

### Good potential here

While some houses may be close to or over the edge of poverty, others present great opportunities — in these circumstances, the symbol would be displayed by hobos lucky enough to have sampled good fortune there. This could refer to an owner who has a lot of work to offer, and possibly some generous accommodation.

### Good railroad jump point

The perception of the hobo is inextricably linked with the railroad, and with good reason, for at one time there were thousands of hobos traveling in boxcars, looking for work or just "moving on." To successfully jump on a train without being spotted requires a certain amount of experience or good luck. If the train is traveling too fast, there is a serious risk of injury, and if the hobo jumps on when it is going slowly he may be seen and thrown off. Knowing where to wait is therefore very useful.

### Good road

This sign would be marked at a crossroads or junction and would be intended to help hobos who were new to the area to choose which way to go. It may indicate that there is work to be had, or that there are friendly locals and generous benefactors to be found along the way.

### Hostile cops

The quality of life of a hobo in a given location is to a certain extent governed by the attitude of the local law enforcement officers: aggressive and overzealous policemen can cause a great deal of trouble, and some may be extremely violent. The feelings of townsfolk are often influenced by past incidents— if a hobo caused trouble in the past, no one ever forgets it, and this is often expressed by the actions of the police.

### Hostile laws and locals

Many hobos relish traveling to places they've never been to before—one of the joys of being on the road—however, this also has its risks. In some places, hobos may pass through without a problem, but in others there may be local ordinances that prohibit vagrancy and are vigorously enforced by the authorities. Knowing what a hobo is going to face before he enters a town can save him from a lot of unnecessary trouble, so this sign is an important one.

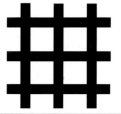

### House temporarily empty

In most cases, the sign for the owner of a property being out is only relevant for a short time. How a hobo reacts to this sign depends on his own ethics and needs. Helping himself to water from a well is not likely to test his conscience, but stealing food or property is against the principles of many hobos— although the best of men still need to eat.

### Jail

The hobo sign for a jail or prison is one of the few where the meaning is clear: it is represented by a set of bars in the form of a grid. There are many reasons why a hobo might want to know that there is a prison nearby—he may want to visit a friend who has been locked up, or he might want to avoid becoming an inmate by keeping a low profile.

### Keep moving

This is a straightforward message to all hobos to keep going until they are out of the area. The symbol is similar to that for "take this direction" but is made more urgent by having twin arrows pointing away. It may indicate the presence of a vindictive sheriff or other law enforcement personnel or dangerous locals. Alternatively, there could be virulent sickness in the area, or even danger from wild animals.

### Kind man here

The sign that a kind gentleman occupies a particular property is always a welcome one. A tired and hungry hobo need not waste time and effort approaching houses where he is likely to be turned away if he is alerted to a good one where he is going to be given food and perhaps shelter. It is also not worth risking trying to steal some food if the owner would give it away willingly in the first place.

### Kind woman here

Every hobo likes to find a house with a generous occupant, and where such places are owned by a kind lady, they are marked with the sign of a cat. This signifies the peace and tranquility of a matronly domesticity and the possibility of a warm meal, perhaps even with a nice warm fire and a purring cat sitting in one's lap.

### Lawman's house

The sign that an officer of the law lives in a particular house can be useful in two main ways. First, any hobo with bad intent is likely to move on rather than risk the wrath of the law; and second, sometimes the officer's assistance is needed, such as when a hobo has been badly injured or has become the victim of a crime—a not uncommon occurrence.

### Make Bible talk

It is obvious why this symbol takes the form of the cross. Where some people will give assistance in response to a sad story, others will welcome a religious traveler. For the ploy to meet with success, it helps if the hobo knows a little of the Bible and is able to convey a Christian ethic and reasonable manners.

### Move on—too many hobos

When they are few and far between, hobos usually find that they are kindly received by the majority of ordinary folk. But it only takes a small number of others to arrive in an area before locals will change their attitude dramatically, especially if they have had property stolen. To find a sign saying that a particular road is full of other hobos can save a lot of time and effort for a tired and hungry traveler.

### Noisy dog

If a hobo desperately needs food or water, especially if it is late at night or early in the morning, they may not want to wait to ask the owners of a property for permission to use a well or take some eggs from a chicken run. At such times, the last thing the hobo wants is for a barking dog to rouse the owners, who may respond to an intruder with a hail of bullets. In such circumstances, a sign to warn of a barking dog may be very useful.

## OK

The range of symbols required to convey meaningful messages is vast, and the simplest of them, like the sign for "OK," may be all that is necessary to mark something out in the desired manner. The cross mark could be put next to a town sign, for instance, to indicate that it is worth entering, or it could be made next to a spring to show that the water there is fit to drink.

## Sad story will get you food

This sign conveys the message that if the right approach is taken, generosity will be forthcoming, probably in the form of food and a warm drink. Many folk will help out a hungry hobo if they have reason to do so—in this case a sad tale is what is required to be invited into the kitchen.

## Safe place and clean water

A traveling hobo would regularly perform a search for safe shelter with a nearby supply of clean water—his efforts would be rewarded if he found this symbol. It is represented by two circles with a cross between them, indicating a safe place, and above them is a wavy line that represents water.

  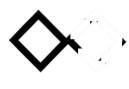

### Say nothing!

Sometimes a traveling hobo will come upon a town where the locals will take almost anything as a provocation for trouble or violence—in such places it is usually wise for him to say nothing and keep his head down. In these circumstances, hobos who had already passed through would find a suitable position somewhere near the town's limits to display this symbol.

### Secure and protected

The sign for a well-guarded house is displayed to warn other hobos that approaching a particular house is likely to be met with aggression, and that it would not be a good idea to enter the property to use a well or to look for food. Since hobos are not constrained by modern lifestyles, they are likely to wander around looking for opportunities for finding clean water or easy food when "normal" folk are asleep. If a house is known to be well-guarded, it can be passed by for a simpler alternative.

### Silence!

The symbol for "silence" is used in a similar way as that for "say nothing." It is marked in places where it is better to pass through unnoticed. Some hobos make noise as they walk, by singing or playing a musical instrument, or several hobos traveling together may talk and laugh loudly. This sign will warn them not to make noise in the area.

## Someone here

If a hobo needs food or water, it's always helpful to know that the owner of a property is in: it may help him avoid getting shot, for one thing. If the hobo's intention is honorable, he'll take a direct approach at the front door; if not, he'll take this as a sign to wait around until the owner leaves or goes to bed before entering the property.

## Stop!

The symbol for "stop!" is usually used to warn other hobos not to continue on their way. This may be because there are bad things ahead— a serious crime may have been committed, there may be a police roadblock across the road, or there may have been a natural disaster of some sort, such as a flood, landslide, forest fire, or earthquake.

## Take this direction

When a hobo is traveling, he may come to a choice of directions; a sign indicating which way to go would be very useful and could prevent time and effort being wasted in taking the wrong road. The reason for indicating a particular direction may be because there are good things to be had there, or because the other road leads to a bad place.

### Trolley bus stop

While most hobos make their journeys by traveling on foot or by jumping onto railroad cars, many also use trolley buses for short trips across towns. Although it normally costs money to do so, some trolley operators follow the same ethic as many railroad workers and let hobos travel for free. In most cases this is just a convenient way of crossing a city; sometimes there is a more urgent reason to pass through quickly and without meeting trouble.

### Unsure of this place

When a hobo marks a symbol for others to see, the status of a given house or town may not be completely certain, for whatever reason. In this case, a single line indicates that the situation is doubtful. Other hobos who then found that the place was in fact OK could indicate this by adding another line to make it into a cross; if they found it was dangerous, they could add two more lines to turn it into the "danger" sign.

### Waste of time

Just because a person lives in a house, it does not mean that they have anything to give a hungry hobo. During the Great Depression, for instance, many families lived on the edge of starvation; indeed many hobos themselves were people who lost their houses through economic hardship, and found they had to go on the road in an attempt to find temporary work. The symbol of an empty circle indicates a house with nothing to give.

### Watch out—troublemaker here

When a tired and hungry hobo is looking for food or work, the last thing he wants is to find that he's been banging on the door of a man with a bad temper; one never knows when such a man will turn violent. Where an unpleasant person has been encountered, a sign is often displayed to warn fellow hobos not to make the same mistake.

### Wealthy folk here

When a hobo finds a sign indicating that the people in a particular house are rich, it warns him how to behave. A bit of planning—washing up, coming up with a sad story, showing good manners, perhaps offering to do some work—is more likely to be rewarded by rich folk than straightforward begging. Knowing what to expect is always valuable on the road.

### You might get attacked here

A spearhead is used by hobos to indicate that there is the risk of attack, and that it may be necessary to defend oneself. Hobos were the target of unprovoked attacks for many reasons. In some areas, local law enforcement agencies turn a blind eye to such behavior if they see it as a method of discouraging hobos from staying around; indeed, it has even been known for attacks to come from vigilante police officers.

# Scientific and Mathematical Symbols

The world of science and mathematics relies on many symbols to simplify, express, or explain complex theories or problems. Over centuries, an almost universal system of notation for mathematical equations, chemical elements or compounds, astronomy, and related items has been adopted, often derived from older systems.

For instance, today's chemist relies heavily on earlier alchemical tradition, but is also thankful for the highly organized mind of Dmitri Mendeleev (1834–1907), a Russian chemist who first proposed the arrangement of the period table of elements in 1869. He ordered the elements according to their atomic weight and showed patterns of properties. The table, rearranged by British physicist Henry Moseley on the basis of increasing atomic number, allowed scientists to predict the properties of elements that had not been discovered.

Alchemists—early chemists—developed symbols to classify the elements they discovered by experimentation. In the alchemical traditions, four elements are required for life to exist: air, fire, water, and earth. They represented the interconnection of all things and the cycle of birth, life, change, and death. Air is said to feed fire, fire dies by water, water is contained by earth, and earth creates the air. Everything is composed of three parts, known as "principles" or "heavenly substances": salt (the physical body), sulfur (the soul or individual essence), and mercury (the life force).

## Mathematical Symbols

Symbols have been used to represent numbers for over 30,000 years, and around 27,000 years ago geometric shapes were being used by early civilizations. The ancient Egyptians developed a decimal number system around 5000 B.C. and symbols to represent specific numbers around 3400 B.C. Since the knowledge of mathematics has increased, many different symbols have developed to denote particular operations. Many are based on the letters of the Greek alphabet, and others resulted from the incorporation of shorthand notations into general use.

## Aluminum

Aluminum, atomic number 13, is a silvery-white metal that was first discovered in Denmark in 1825 by Hans Christian Oersted. The name derives from the Latin word *alumen,* meaning alum, a substance that was used in medicine by the ancient Greeks and Romans as an astringent. Aluminum is a light, nontoxic metal with important engineering properties, such as being easy to cast and machine. In its pure form, it is too soft for industrial use, but when alloyed with other substances, including copper, magnesium, silicon, and manganese, it becomes an extremely important material.

## Antimony

Antimony, atomic number 51, is a bluish-colored metallic element with a brittle crystalline structure. It was known to ancient cultures; these days it is used for hardening lead, in the production of plastics, and in various chemicals. It is obtained from the minerals stibnite and valentinite, and is highly toxic, as are compounds of antimony. The name is derived from the Greek *anti* (opposed) and *monos* (solitude).

### Arsenic

Arsenic, atomic number 33, occurs in two forms: one is colored yellow, the other gray; both are semimetallic with brittle crystalline structures. It was known to ancient cultures, and was used as a poison for more than 2,000 years. These days it is used in the production of semiconductors—its extreme toxicity limiting the applications to which it could be put. The name is derived from the Latin word *arsenicum* and the Greek word *arsenikos,* as is the symbol As.

### Bismuth

Bismuth, atomic number 83, is a pinkish white metallic element with a brittle crystalline structure. It was known to ancient cultures, and is used for making fuses and in the production of pharmaceutical chemicals. It is obtained from the minerals bismite, bismuthinite, and bismutite; it is the most diamagnetic of all metals, and has a rhombohedral crystal structure. The name is derived from the German word *wissmuth* (white mass), as is the symbol Bi.

## Carbon

Carbon, atomic number 6, is a nonmetallic element that occurs in many forms, which are known as isotopes; two well-known examples are graphite and diamond. Carbon has been known to mankind as charcoal, soot, and coal for thousands of years, although it was not understood that it was an element until more recent times. The name originates from the Latin word *carbo,* which means "charcoal." Carbon is a vital component in nature, and is widely distributed throughout the universe, being found in the sun, stars, planets, and comets.

## Cobalt

Cobalt, atomic number 27, is a hard, brittle, silvery grayish metal that was discovered in Sweden in 1735 by Georg Brandt. It is magnetic, and belongs to a group of elements known as transition metals. Its name derives from the German word *kobald,* which means goblin or evil spirit. It was known in mineral salt form to ancient cultures from the Middle East, where it was used to impart a beautiful dark blue color to glass. Cobalt is found in meteorites, although it is obtained commercially from ore deposits in Zaire, Morocco, and Canada.

### Copper

Copper, atomic number 29, is a reddish metallic element that polishes to a bright shine. It was known to ancient cultures and was first used more than 4,000 years ago to make bronze for weapons and other artifacts. Through the ages it has been used for many different purposes, including making buckets, plumbing fittings, and ornamental features. Nowadays it is used for making coins, jewelry, and many electrical items. Both the name and symbol, Cu, are derived from the Latin word *cyprium,* after the island of Cyprus. It is obtained from several minerals, including chalcopyrite and malachite.

### Gold

Gold, atomic number 79, is a yellowish metallic element that polishes to a bright shine. It is thought to have been discovered around 5,000 years ago; since it occurs naturally in nature, it is certainly possible that it was known well before this. It has been used ever since in the construction of jewelry, coinage, and valuable artifacts, and today it is used in electronic components. The name comes from the Old English word *geolu,* which means yellow, and the symbol, Au, comes from the Latin word *aurum,* or gold.

## Hydrogen

Hydrogen, atomic number 1, is the lightest gas known: it is colorless and odorless, and was discovered in London in 1766 by Henry Cavendish. The name hydrogen was applied by the French chemist Lavoisier, and derives from the Greek words *hydro* and *genes*, which mean "water" and "generator." Since it is lighter than air, hydrogen was originally used in commercial balloons. Many lives were lost in tragic accidents due to its inflammable nature, however, and it is no longer used for this purpose, having been replaced by helium.

## Iron

Iron, atomic number 26, is a silver-colored metallic element that was known to ancient cultures. It is a vital constituent of mammalian blood—red blood cells contain hemoglobin, which is an iron-based molecule used to carry oxygen around the body. The name and symbol, Fe, are derived from the Latin word *ferrum*. Its primary use is in the manufacture of steel; it is obtained from several iron ores, such as the mineral hematite.

## Lead

Lead, atomic number 82, is a bluish-silver-colored metallic element that was known to ancient cultures, who used it to manufacture all manner of objects including drinking vessels and plumbing systems—which was unfortunate, as it is highly toxic. The symbol Pb comes from the Latin word *plumbum,* which means lead. These days it is used for making solder, rainwater shielding for houses, and batteries; it is obtained from the mineral ore galena.

## Magnesium

Magnesium, atomic number 12, is a gray-colored metallic element that tarnishes rapidly when exposed to air. Although it is the eighth most common element in the earth's crust, it was not until 1808 that it was discovered by Sir Humphry Davy. It is a lightweight metal with excellent engineering properties, which have made it popular in the aerospace, defense, and motor racing industries. It is obtained from seawater, and the name is derived from the city of Magnesia, as is the symbol, Mg.

## Mercury

Mercury, atomic number 80, is the heaviest known elemental liquid. It was known to ancient cultures, who called it "quicksilver" after the manner in which it moves. This association with rapid movement led it to be renamed after the Roman god Mercury, known for his speed as a messenger. The symbol Hg is derived from the Latin word *hydrargyrum,* which means liquid silver. It is obtained from a mineral ore called cinnabar, and is used for many different purposes, including for thermometers, barometers, fluorescent lamps, and batteries.

## Nitrogen

Nitrogen, atomic number 7, symbol N, is a colorless, odorless, and mostly inert gas that makes up about 78 percent of the earth's atmosphere. It was discovered in 1772 in Scotland by Daniel Rutherford, and its name is from the Greek words *nitron* and *genes,* which mean "niter forming"—niter, or potassium nitrate, being an important chemical used in the manufacture of gunpowder. Compounds of nitrogen are used in fertilizers, foods, and many other commercial chemical processes, and are vital to all forms of life. Many plants take nitrogen from the atmosphere and convert it into forms that end up in the soil; this process is extremely important in agriculture and is called "fixing."

**Scientific and Mathematical Symbols**

### Oxygen

Oxygen, atomic number 8, symbol O, is a colorless, odorless gas that forms about 20 percent of the earth's atmosphere. It was discovered independently in England and Sweden in 1774 by Joseph Priestley and Carl Scheele. The name originates from the Greek words *oxy* and *genes,* which mean "acid forming." It is a very reactive element, and is a vital component for the respiration of animals and plants—it is also necessary for most forms of combustion. Oxygen makes up about 66 percent of the human body.

### Phosphorus

Phosphorus, atomic number 15, symbol P, is a nonmetallic element that catches fire on exposure to air. It occurs in three forms: white (or yellow), red, and black. It is a vital component of living things, and was first discovered in 1669 by Hennig Brand, when it was shown that certain compounds glowed in the dark. As a result of this luminescence, its name was derived from the Greek words *phôs,* meaning light, and *phoros,* meaning bearer. It is used in the manufacture of fertilizers and detergents, and is obtained from phosphate rock.

## Platinum

Platinum, atomic number 78, is a silver-white-colored precious metal that was discovered in 1735 by Julius Scaliger. The name and symbol Pt are derived from the Spanish word *platina*, which means "little silver," and it is used for making jewelry, for specialist containers for the chemical industry, and for catalytic converters for the automotive market. It is obtained from mineral ores as part of the process of mining silver and gold.

## Potassium

Potassium, atomic number 19, is a silver-white-colored alkali metal that was discovered in 1807 by Sir Humphry Davy; it is the seventh most abundant element in the earth's crust. It is a vital component in the chemistry of most living things. The name is derived from the word *potash*, and the symbol K comes from the Latin word *kalium*. It is used for making glass and soap, and is obtained from various minerals including carnallite.

### Silver

Silver, atomic number 47, is a white metallic element that was known to ancient cultures. The name is derived from the Old English word *seolfor,* meaning silver, and the symbol Ag comes from the Latin word *argentum,* which also means silver. It has been used for making valuable items like jewelry for at least 5,000 years, and these days it is used in manufacturing photographic chemicals and electrical conductors. Although it occasionally occurs naturally as native silver, it is generally obtained when mining gold and platinum.

### Sodium

Sodium, atomic number 11, is a silvery-white metal that was first discovered in 1807 in England by Sir Humphry Davy. The name sodium originates from the English word *soda,* but the symbol, Na, derives from the Latin word *natrium.* It is a member of the group of alkali metals, and is most commonly found as salt (sodium chloride). It was not until the eighteenth century that sodium and potassium were recognized as being distinct from each other, since they have very similar properties. Sodium is a vital component in most living things.

## Sulfur

Sulfur, atomic number 16, symbol S, is a brittle, pale-yellow-colored nonmetallic element that has been known for thousands of years. It occurs naturally in a pure form around the vent pipes of volcanoes, but also as various compounds such as Epsom salts. Many sulfur compounds are extremely toxic. The name is derived from the Latin word *sulfur,* which means brimstone. It is used for making many things, including matches, gunpowder, and medicines.

## Tin

Tin, atomic number 50, is a silvery-white colored element with a crystalline structure. It was known to ancient cultures, who combined it with copper to make bell metals. It has been speculated that it was first found when rocks containing cassiterite were accidentally burned while they were being used around cooking fires. The name and symbol Sn are derived from the Latin word *stannum,* which means tin. It is used for plating food cans due to its anticorrosion properties.

### Air

Air is the first element of the alchemical tradition and represents the essence of intuition and learning; it is regarded as the "element of the North" and the "nature of the mind." Further attributes include the archetypal property of carrying the spirit into the manifested world. It is associated with the astrological signs Gemini, Libra, and Aquarius, and is represented by the metal iron, as well as by feathers, birds, incense, fans, flags, flowing garments, and sheer material.

### Fire

Fire is the second element of the alchemical tradition and represents the essence of purification and change; it is regarded as the "element of the East" and the "nature of the will." Further attributes include the archetypal properties of activity and transformation. It is associated with the astrological signs Aries, Leo, and Sagittarius, and is represented by the metal lead, as well as by fire, candles, lights, dragons, and the sun.

## Water

Water is the third element of the alchemical tradition and represents the essence of love and fertility; it is regarded as the "element of the South" and the "nature of emotions." It is associated with the astrological signs Cancer, Scorpio, and Pisces. Further attributes include the archetypal properties of cleansing and purification; it is primarily represented by the metal tin, but also by lavender fragrance, fish, coral, and sponges.

## Earth

Earth is the fourth element of the alchemical tradition and represents the essence of grounding and stability; it is regarded as the "element of the West" and the "nature of balance." It is associated with the astrological signs Taurus, Virgo, and Capricorn. Further attributes include the archetypal properties of manifestation, birth, and material creation; it is represented by the mineral malachite, the green ore of copper.

### Amalgam

An early symbol for amalgam and much used by alchemists. An amalgam is a mixture of metal (often gold) with mercury to make an alloy. Its composition has been known and used since classical times. Gold amalgam was used in Renaissance times for gilding furniture and decorative items such as picture frames. Copper, zinc, gold, and tin amalgam are also used by dentists for filling and strengthening teeth.

### Aqua fortis

Pure aqua fortis is a scentless and colorless liquid, known to ancient alchemists as "strong water." It is known to modern-day chemists as nitric acid. It was usually made by distilling green vitriol with saltpeter and alum, although this often resulted in a smelly brown liquid due to the presence of impurities. When made properly, aqua fortis is a strong corrosive acid that reacts vigorously with most substances, including all the metals known to alchemists, except gold, which is unaffected by it.

### Aqua regia

Aqua regia is a mixture of one part aqua fortis (nitric acid) and three or four parts "spirit of salt" (hydrochloric acid). Since this mixture would dissolve the king of all metals, gold—a material that was unaffected by any other acid—it was called "aqua regia," which means "king's water." Once its properties were discovered, it became a key part of the alchemist's tool kit, since substances containing dissolved gold were thought to have special qualities.

## Borax

Borax occurs naturally as a deposit from the evaporation of alkaline lakes and appears as a white powder or as crystals. Chemically it is hydrated sodium borate. It was important in the early tanning industry and later became useful as a cleansing agent in the manufacture of enamels, glass, and porcelain. In more recent times it has been used as a water softener and cleanser. It is an important source of boron, a rare element.

## Brimstone

Due to its dreadful smell and virulent bright yellow color, brimstone was popularly believed to be the fuel on which the fires of hell burned. This belief was strengthened by the fact that it is found around hot springs and in areas of recent volcanic activity. The more modern name for brimstone is sulfur. When brimstone oxidizes it becomes sulfuric acid, which used to be known as oil of vitriol or simply vitriol.

## Caput mortuum

A general term used by early alchemists to signify the residual matter remaining after a substance had been heated until all its volatile components vaporized. The expression was also used to specifically refer to a substance known as "Venetian red." This was a deep red-brown coloring pigment of ferric (iron) oxide, which was prepared synthetically by "calcining ferrous sulfate in the presence of lime." This basically means heating iron sulfate with limestone, the residue of which was called *caput mortuum,* Latin for "head of the dead."

### Cinnabar

Mercury, a great favorite of ancient alchemists, was usually obtained from the bright red mineral ore cinnabar, which was roasted over a fire until the pure metal oozed out and was collected. Modern-day chemists refer to it as mercury sulfide, but ancient cultures called it "dragon's blood," since it gave off thick red smoke during the roasting process. Cinnabar represents the terrestrial marriage of the soul and spirit of substances: these have to be separated to free the essences that are then used for alchemical practices.

### Essential oil

Also known as ethereal oil, this naturally volatile oil is secreted by aromatic plants, especially ones from hot, dry environments such as rosemary and lavender. Apothecaries valued essential oils for their strong aroma, a drop of which was needed for mixing into exotic perfumes like oil of attar and patchouli. It takes a large quantity of plant material to produce even a small amount of oil, so it was then and is now a very valuable resource, and has been prized since time immemorial.

### Glass

Some of the earliest glass is Roman in origin. Glass is made from the fusion of calcium oxide (lime), sodium carbonate (soda), and silicon dioxide (silica). The quality of glass improved over the centuries as scientists better understood how to make it stronger and clearer. Glass was very important in scientific discovery, as early scientists learned to grind glass into lenses, which in turn enabled the development of better instruments like microscopes and telescopes.

## Hematite

This is an ancient sign for hematite, a common oxide of iron, and the principal source of iron ore. Powdered hematite has been used since classical times as red ocher by artists and fresco painters. Hematite is found in sedimentary strata across the world. It can occur as beautiful rhombohedral crystals that are found particularly on the island of Elba, or more commonly as kidney ore when it comes in the form of dark brown nodules.

## Litharge

Litharge is a rare mineral of pale yellow or reddish yellow color. Alchemists knew of only a few restricted locations where it could be found, in certain parts of Scandinavia. Modern chemists refer to it as either lead monoxide or lead protoxide: it has been used for many years as a reddish yellow pigment, for which it has been given the name "lead ocher." It has also been used extensively in the manufacture of flint glass, batteries, and for glazing earthenware.

## Marcasite

Marcasite is just one of the many naturally occurring forms of iron pyrites, also known as "fool's gold." It can be found either as hard yellow cubic crystals resembling brass, or as brown nodular lumps that gleam with golden hues when broken open. It was wrongly thought by some alchemists that marcasite was partly made up of arsenic. Chemically, it is known as iron disulfide, although in the past that term was sometimes used to refer to bismuth, which is an unrelated substance.

### Mercury

Mercury, the third alchemic principle, represents the "integrative force," interweaving and balancing salt and sulfur. Known to ancient cultures as quicksilver, it could be found seeping from cracks in certain rocks, and also could be extracted from the mineral cinnabar by roasting. Mercury was often converted into various compounds, such as the highly toxic white mercuric oxide and the slightly less poisonous red mercuric oxide.

### Niter

Niter is known to modern chemists as potassium nitrate, but formerly it was also called saltpeter. It was used by alchemists through the ages to make nitric acid, which they knew as aqua fortis, or "strong water." It was produced by a process called lixiviation, in which a pile of soil rich in animal dung was left under cover but open to the air until a crust of niter formed.

### Oil

There are many forms of oil in alchemy—plant oils, animal oils, and mineral oils such as oil of tartar, oil of realgar, oil of vitriol, and so on. Oils obtained from plants are called essential oils; these volatile oils are obtained in small but very strong amounts and are extracted from aromatic plants like rosemary, patchouli, attar, and lavender. Edible oils also come from plants and are widely used in foods and cosmetics. The principal ones come from olives, sunflowers, soy beans, maize, and coconuts.

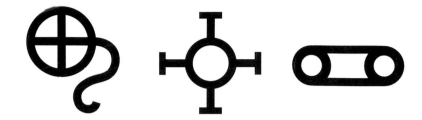

### Oil of vitriol

Oil of vitriol was an important ingredient in alchemy; modern chemists know it as sulfuric acid, and it is one of the strongest of the mineral acids. It has to be handled with great care, as it is an extremely corrosive substance. These days it is sometimes also referred to as battery acid. Alchemists used to make it by distilling a solution of iron sulfate, which due to the color of the crystal form was known as green vitriol.

### Olive oil

This edible pale yellow or green natural oil is the extract of the fruit of the *Olea europaea* tree found growing all over the Mediterranean. The oil is extracted by pressing the olives between heavy weights and has been an essential foodstuff for Mediterranean cultures for millennia.

### Orpiment

Another mineral ore of arsenic, orpiment sometimes goes by the name auripigment. It has a bright yellow color that has made it a popular choice for producing pigments for use in paints, where it is referred to as "king's yellow." Modern chemists know this substance as arsenic trisulfide, and like many other pigments it is highly toxic. Orpiment retains its yellow coloration more than realgar, which in time fades from red to orange.

### Ounce

This is the pharmaceutical symbol for an ounce. An apothecaries' ounce weighs 480 grains, or one twelfth of a pound troy. Troy weights are named after the town of Troyes in France, where the weights were standardized for precious metals and gems: a pound is twelve ounces or 5,760 grains. When followed by an "i," the symbol indicates one ounce; with the addition of "ss" it signifies half an ounce. Therefore, an ounce and a half is shown with the symbol followed by "iss." Two ounces is shown by the ounce symbol followed by "ij."

### Precipitation

There are various chemical procedures that form the mainstay of alchemy, and one of these is precipitation. This is a process whereby a reaction is instigated in a liquid or mix of liquids, a result of which is the appearance of small particles of solid material; these then "fall out" of the solution, and form a layer at the bottom of the reaction vessel. The reaction was known to alchemists as "coagulation," and the material produced was (and still is) known as "precipitate."

### Quicklime

Quicklime is a white powder known to modern chemists as calcium oxide. It can be obtained by heating limestone, egg shells, or any material containing chalk. Once formed, quicklime becomes very reactive to any moisture, and is a strong desiccating (drying) agent. When exposed to water it produces slaked lime, which is used for many purposes including making lime mortar for building houses. It is also a powerful chemical agent, and reacts strongly when mixed with many other substances and heated.

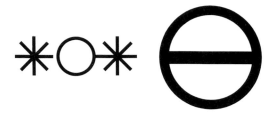

### Realgar

Realgar is a mineral ore of arsenic and is the major source for its production. It is a brittle red vitreous or crystalline solid, which sublimates like sal ammoniac. Modern chemists know it as arsenic disulfide, and it has been used for centuries as a pigment in paints. It has also been used for many years as a coloring agent in fireworks, especially in China. The similarities in its structure and that of sulfur has resulted in the nickname "ruby sulfur." It was probably first found around the vents of volcanoes or in hot spring deposits, since it crystallizes out of volcanic vapors. Its name comes from the Arabic words for "powder of the mine."

### Sal ammoniac

Sal ammoniac is a white powdery material that is known to modern chemists as ammonium chloride; its name derives from the place it was originally made: the Temple of Jupiter at Ammon in Egypt. When heated it turns into a white vapor and then condenses into a solid form as it cools. This process, known as sublimation, was considered an important part of alchemy.

### Salt

One of the three principles of alchemy, salt represents the final manifestation of the "perfected stone" of alchemy. It is considered to be the "contractive force" in nature; it is associated with the operations of crystallization and condensation. Salt is said to be connected to the action of thought on matter, including that of the process of meditation performed by alchemists to transform materials. Salt (sodium chloride) was also known by alchemists to have the property of reducing decay.

### Saltpeter

This is an early chemical sign for potassium nitrate. This form of potassium nitrate occurs naturally. It is an important constituent of the gunpowder used in explosives. A white crystalline substance, it is a strong oxidizing agent. It is used medicinally and in the manufacture of glass. It is an old-fashioned meat preservative.

### Scruple

A scruple is an apothecaries' measure of weight equal to twenty grains or one third of a dram. Many medicines are so potent that they are used in only the very tiniest amounts—such as one scruple—and have to be weighed on very sensitive instruments. To indicate one scruple, the symbol is shown followed by an "i"; to show half a scruple, "ss" is added to the right of the symbol.

### Spirit

Alchemists considered life a vital essence—that is, a substance independent from bodily existence that was the "active presence in all of us that strives toward perfection." It was also thought that spirits would seek to express themselves by manifesting themselves in a material form. Spirits could be represented by any of the three principles—sulfur, salt, or quicksilver (mercury). There were those who also included arsenic or orpiment as spirit substances.

### Steel

This is the most commonly used metal in the world. It is a metal alloy made from iron with a little added carbon for strength. With tempering (hammering) it can be made to various degrees of hardness. In ancient times it could only be made in small amounts by heating cast iron to reduce the carbon on the surface; the blacksmith would then shape and temper the steel into implements and weapons such as swords. When technology improved, steel was made in crucibles, although still in small quantities, until the Industrial Revolution when methods for mass production were developed.

### Sublimation

Sublimation was another of the primary operations of alchemy. This process was observed when certain solids were heated and their vapors solidified as they cooled. An example of such a material is sal ammoniac, which was known by the earliest alchemists to behave in this manner. Due to the precise manner in which sublimation occurs, this process was sometimes associated with the astrological symbol of weighing scales, which is the sign for the constellation of Libra.

### Sulfur

Sulfur is the second of the three alchemic principles: it represents the "expansive force" in nature, and is associated with passion and will. It is also connected with the operation of fermentation. It was said by ancient cultures that sulfur was produced by the "dry exhalations of the earth"; since it forms around volcanic vents, this is an understandable view. Some alchemists believed that sulfur removed all traces of poison from arsenic and antimony, which would have proved fatal to those who believed them. It was also thought that essential oils found in plants represented the presence of sulfur.

### Talc

This lovely old symbol signified talc, which is also known as soapstone or steatite. Powdered talc has been used by people for millennia as a cosmetic for smoothing and softening the skin. It is a very soft, hydrous magnesium silicate mineral formed in metamorphic rocks and found in particularly large deposits in India and Austria. As well as being used in the cosmetic industry, talc is used in paper making, paint, rubber, and textiles.

### Tartar

Tartar is a substance known to modern chemists as potassium hydrogen tartrate. It was originally obtained as a by-product of the wine making process, scraped from the insides of wine barrels. It was often then used to make a powerful emetic for medicinal use, by reacting it with calcined antimony. The resulting chemical was known as "tartar emetic," which although popular, had to be administered with great care as it was highly poisonous.

### Universal seed

Universal seed was considered by alchemists to be the source of all life. There were two forms of seed: The primary one was the "Universal, Superior, and Masculine Seed," which was considered to be the "sulfur of Nature, the first and most Potent cause of all Generation." The secondary form was the "Universal, Inferior, and Feminine Seed," which was thought to be carried in the "belly of the wind." It was said to be possible to extract universal seed from rainwater.

### Urine

Urine has been used in the tanning industry as a bleaching agent since the earliest times. A pale yellow mixture of water and uric acid, urine is waste matter excreted by the kidneys and then expelled from the body as a useless toxic liquid. Urine is species, diet, and environment specific.

### Vinegar

Vinegar is a mild form of acid that is made from the oxidization of fruit or vegetable matter. Its sharp taste is used in cooking as a flavor enhancer, and it is a food preservative; it was much used before the development of the refrigerator. Vinegar is produced when alcohol is oxidized by bacteria so that the ethanol converts to acetic (ethanoic) acid. This process occurs naturally to alcohol when it is left exposed to the open air. Vinegar can be made from a variety of sources such as red wine, white wine, and cider.

### Wax

Wax has been important since earliest times, principally for the manufacture of candles but also for its use in casting—as in the lost wax process. Wax is secreted by honeybees when they are making honeycomb cells for storing the honey they make. Pure wax is a soft golden color with a pleasant aroma. Easily liquefied by warming, wax has been used for waterproofing clothing and for sealing other materials since earliest times. It is also an important ingredient in wood and floor polishes.

### Annual

An annual is a plant that germinates from a seed, grows, flowers, sets seed (or fruit), then dies—all within one season. Perhaps the most obvious symbolic example is the poppy but there are a number of others such as the marigold or Cempazu-chiles in Mexican. Mexicans associate these bright orange and yellow flowers with death and use them for decoration during the Day of the Dead.

### Biennial

A biennial is a plant that germinates and starts growing in its first season, lives through the winter, then uses its stored food to grow to maturity, flower, and then set seed (or fruit) before dying. A biennial lives for a total of two years. Examples of biennials include flowers such as hollyhocks, sweet William, and foxgloves as well as a number of important vegetable crops such as artichoke, carrot, parsnip, turnips, and celery.

### Bush

The botanical definition of a bush is a low-growing perennial plant with multiple branches that arise from the same growing place. Bushes are less significant than trees in myth; the most notable is the burning bush of biblical fame, a thorny acacia. According to the Bible, Moses was on Mount Sinai when he saw a bush in flames that never burned up. He took this as a sign from god and in reverence to the Holy Spirit he removed his sandals—as Muslims also do when they enter a mosque.

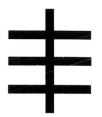  

### Deadly

Many of the most deadly poisons in the world occur naturally in plants, such as tobacco (nicotine), foxglove (digitalis), giant hogweed (hemlock), aconite (aconitum), and dieffenbachia (strychnine). Such plants have their uses in drugs and as fungicides and herbicides, but they must always be handled with great care. It is vitally important that such plants are clearly labeled— their misuse would be fatal.

### Dioecious

Most plants carry both male and female parts (they are monoecious) and can produce pollen and seeds. However, the plants of some species are either male or female. These dioecious plants need a plant of each sex growing close by before they can set seed. The advantage of this is that it ensures genetic variability; the disadvantage is that more than one plant of a species is needed for reproduction. It is horticulturally and commercially important to know which sex the plant is.

### Infinite number of petals

Each petal on a flower is technically an individual unit of the corolla. Most flower species produce a set number of petals depending on the variety. However, some flowers produce erratic numbers of multiple petals, which vary not only from plant to plant but from flower to flower. This information is important for the botanist to know but is also crucial for plant breeders attempting to improve the flower by hybridizing.

**Scientific and Mathematical Symbols**

### Mineral kingdom

This is the symbol for mineralia (the mineral kingdom) and dates from the eighteenth century. Minerals are generally naturally occurring inorganic substances that typically have a crystalline structure. Each mineral can be identified by its characteristic chemical composition as well as by its hardness, color, luster, fracture, and relative density. Mineralia was the collective term used by scientists for all minerals in general—the equivalent terms were vegetabilia, meaning belonging to the plant kingdom, and animalia, belonging to the animal kingdom.

### Perennial

A perennial plant lives for more than two seasons and can in fact live for many years. Many herbs are perennials and they are significant in myths and legends, for example, rosemary—which means "dew of the sea"—is a highly aromatic plant that was sacred to Dionysus and Aphrodite. For the ancient Greeks and Romans rosemary was a symbol of remembrance and faithfulness between lovers. It was also symbolic of fertility and longevity and was used at funerals as a symbol of immortality.

### Pernicious

Pernicious plants are invasive and destructive of other plants' habitats. They can destroy other species and sometimes carry a growth inhibitor that affects other plants around them. Such plants are often alien introductions that have no natural predator in their new environment. Many national and state governments issue lists of banned and pernicious plants that are illegal to grow or propagate.

## Poisonous

This symbol is used to indicate a poisonous plant. Many common ornamental plants grown in domestic gardens are toxic when eaten in quantity and should be handled with care. Traditionally apothecaries and pharmacists have used such plants for the benefits that small, carefully measured doses can confer. The poison can suffuse the whole plant or occur in just the sap, the roots, or the leaves. Some plants such as foxgloves and aconites are highly toxic and should be labeled to alert the unwary gardener.

## Tree

The botanical definition of a tree is a perennial plant with a single woody stem or trunk that is unbranched for some distance off the ground. Trees usually live for many decades, with some species such as yew living for centuries. Some of the oldest living things are trees. Because of their impressive size and age trees are mythologically important in many cultures and are often directly involved in the creation myth.

## Wood

Wood is the earliest material known to man and probably the most versatile, providing everything from houses and shelter to tools, boats, and crockery. Depending on the type of tree—hardwood or softwood—the composition and qualities vary from species to species. Generally speaking, the slower growing trees yield denser, harder quality wood than fast growing trees. Depending on the use for the wood, carvers and carpenters each have their preferred type.

Scientific and Mathematical Symbols

### Mercury

The symbol for the planet Mercury represents the winged-helmet messenger of the gods in both Greek and Roman mythology. This is probably because this planet moves quickly as it orbits the sun. It is associated with many things that reflect speed: transportation, commerce, and thievery. The Greeks gave it two names: for its appearance as the morning star, they called it Apollo, and as the evening star, Hermes.

### Venus

The symbol for the planet Venus represents the cross of spirit under the circle of life. Venus was the Roman goddess of love and beauty, and is synonymous with the Greek goddess Aphrodite and the Babylonian Ishtar. It is considered by many to be the planet of love, and apart from the sun and moon, it is the brightest object in the sky. It has had significance to humankind in rituals and religion since prehistoric times, and has been called many things over the years, including "Jewel of the Sky."

## Earth

The symbol for the planet Earth is composed of the cross of life superimposed on a circle that represents our home planet. This symbolizes the fact that the Earth is the planet we live on. The Earth was believed to be flat by most western Europeans until scientists started to make accurate measurements of the stars, and worked out that the Earth must be round; Greek scientists knew this nearly 2,000 years earlier.

## Mars

The symbol for the planet Mars represents both the sun and an arrow—this reflects the fact that in late Roman mythology it was associated with Mars, the god of war; and was considered to be very much a male sign. The twin attributes of survival and energy are bound up with this planet, and the fact that it is red meant that it often symbolized anger and warriorlike actions.

### Jupiter

The symbol for the planet Jupiter represents branches reaching out from an inner cross, which denotes the soul. In Roman mythology, Jupiter defended the city of Rome from enemy invaders using thunderbolts to drive them away. He also oversaw warriors going off to war and then coming back from the field of battle. It is the biggest planet in the solar system, and this has made it fascinating to observers since ancient times.

### Saturn

The symbol for the planet Saturn is represented by the cross of life and an inward branch—this symbolizes the connection with the inner self, and as a result it has been called the "Planet of Fate" and the "Lord of Karma." The name Saturn comes from the Roman god, known in Greek mythology as Cronos; he was the son of Uranus and Gaia, and the father of Zeus and the Olympians.

## Uranus

This was the first stellar object to be positively identified as a planet: it was discovered in 1781 by William and Caroline Hershel, who saw its distinctive disc through a low-powered telescope. It is named after the father of the Roman god Saturn. Uranus was married to Gaia, and was killed by his jealous son Saturn when he reached manhood as part of Saturn's campaign to remove any threats to his power.

## Neptune

The symbol for the planet Neptune represents the trident of the Roman sea god, Neptune, a deity known by the Greeks as Poseidon. Both were considered to be masters of the waterways, including all rivers, lakes, ponds, and seas. The gods were greatly respected and feared by all who traveled by boat or ship, and offerings to them were often made before leaving shore. The sign of Neptune is also associated with creative arts, such as poetry, artistry, and writing.

### Pluto

The original symbol for the planet Pluto was made up from the initials of the man who first predicted the existence of this tiny astronomical body—Percival Lowell. More recently, a different symbol has been used extensively: this is made up of the cross of life, the circle of boundless infinity, and a semicircle representing the outer aspects of existence. This planet is used in astrology to symbolize the process of death and regeneration, including disease and personal shame.

### Aurora borealis

Also known as the northern lights, these are beautiful bands of red and green (sometimes multicolored) brilliant lights sparkling in arcs and bands across the night sky. They are an upper atmosphere phenomena that occurs in the far northern polar regions. The borealis is caused by high-speed charged solar particles entering the ionosphere and releasing electrons that collide with oxygen and nitrogen atoms in the atmosphere. In the southern hemisphere the effect is called the southern lights or aurora australis.

## Ceres

The asteroid Ceres was first discovered on New Year's Day in 1801. It was the first asteroid to be found, and is also the largest of all the many thousands of objects in a debris belt that orbits between the planets of Mars and Jupiter. The name is that of the Roman earth goddess, Ceres (who was also known to the Greeks as Demeter). She was wife of the god Jupiter (Zeus).

## Juno

When Juno was discovered in 1805, it became the third asteroid to be recorded. It is named after the Roman goddess who was known in Greek mythology as Hera. She was the wife of the god Jupiter (Greek Zeus), and said to be the most beautiful of all the immortals, surpassing even Aphrodite—every spring her beauty was renewed allowing her to retain her looks as she grew older.

### Moon

The symbol for Earth's closest neighbor is a crescent moon. It has been important to human culture since the earliest times, and has had significance in rituals and religions ever since. It was called both Selene and Artemis by the Greeks. The Romans called the moon Luna, from which we get the term lunatic, based on the observation that psychiatric patients were more violent during the full moon than at any other time.

### Pallas

The asteroid Pallas Athene was discovered in 1802, making it only the second of these tiny objects to be found. It is named after the Roman goddess of wisdom, intellect, and invention. She was known in Greek mythology as Minerva, and was the daughter of Zeus. The city of Athens was named after her to honor her love and protection of the great hero Odysseus (Roman Ulysses) in his long and arduous travels.

## Sun

As the source of life itself, the sun has always been an important symbol in every culture and religion. Inevitably it is featured in every creation myth, and the most important god in every pantheon is associated with the sun. This god is usually male with his female counterpart being represented by the moon. The major exception to this is in Japanese culture where the sun is feminine and the moon masculine. In addition, due to the way the sun rises and sets every day, it is also a symbol of death and resurrection.

## Vesta

The asteroid Vesta was discovered in 1807. It was named after the Roman goddess of the hearth fire, and hence the symbol is a flame. In Greek mythology Vesta was known as Hestia and was the eldest sister of Zeus—she was said to be immune to the love spells of Aphrodite, and was able to choose not to marry. Instead she devoted her time to looking after Apollo's dwellings, and was noted for being kind to poor people, for which she was loved by many.

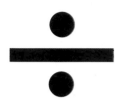

### Division

The symbol for division as shown here is probably of seventeenth-century English origin; before that time it was used in continental Europe to indicate a half, or subtraction, and before that—around the tenth century—it was used as shorthand for the word *est*. It is possible that this is where the division symbol was derived, since the sign was sometimes put after the word *divisa* to mean "is divided."

### Existential quantifier

The ancient Greek philosopher Aristotle laid the foundations of mathematical logic over 2,000 years ago with a system called "categorical logic," where a proposition is made concerning a relationship between two terms. This has since evolved into "predicate logic," which uses a series of expressive symbols to make assertive statements. The existential quantifier is one of these, and is used to state that a particular entity exists.

### Finite difference or increment

The Greek letter delta is used to denote a finite change in a state or quantity, and has been used for this purpose for more than three hundred years by mathematicians and scientists the world over. The symbol D would typically be placed next to the symbol for the quantity that is changing; for instance, "DP" could be used to represent a change in pressure.

# Ω π θ

### Greek letter omega

Omega is the last letter of the Greek alphabet, and in its capital form is used to represent ohm, the SI unit of electrical resistance. This is named after Georg Ohm, a German physicist who discovered by experimentation that there was a relation between voltage and current: this is known today as Ohm's law. In Ohm's law, 1 ohm equals 1 volt divided by 1 ampere.

### Greek letter pi

The symbol pi is one of the most commonly used in mathematics today; it represents the ratio of the circumference to the diameter of a circle. Although the ancient Greeks were familiar with the concept, they did not use the p symbol to represent it. Somewhere around the year 250 B.C., Archimedes wrote a document called "On the Sphere and the Cylinder," in which he gave an approximation of the value of pi, but it was not until A.D. 263 that a Chinese mathematician named Liu Hui specified the actual value of 3.14159. The symbol pi was first adopted to represent the number in 1706 by the English mathematician William Jones.

### Greek letter theta

The Greek letter theta may be used as a variable name, much like x and y, but it is also commonly used as a symbol to denote an angle. Theta is also used in polar coordinates to indicate the "angle coordinate," which is the point designated by (x,y) in the so-called Cartesian coordinate system (invented by and named after René Descartes).

### Infinity

Infinity is defined as "a quantity that is larger than any assignable quantity," and is the result of dividing any number by zero. Although the ancient Greeks knew about and discussed this concept as early as the fifth century B.C., they used the infinity symbol to represent the figure 10,000. The symbol we use today for infinity was first used in print in 1655, in a book titled *Arithmetica Infinitorum,* written by English mathematician John Wallis (1616–1703).

### Integral sign

The symbol for integration (sometimes referred to as "reverse differentiation") was used for the first time by Gottfried Wilhelm Leibniz (1646–1716) on October 29, 1675, in an unpublished manuscript. Later that same year, he proposed its use in a letter to the secretary of the Royal Society. The first time the integral sign was printed was when he published a paper in a journal called *Acta Eruditorum.*

### Is less than or equal to

The two main symbols for "inequality" were first used by the English mathematician Thomas Harriot (1560–1621) in his great work entitled *Artis Analyticae Praxis,* published in London in 1631. This book dealt with the theory of equations, and in it Harriot made use of the symbols ">" for "is greater than" and "<" for "is less than". When the symbol is underscored, it modifies the meaning to include "or equal to"—so, for instance, the symbol "≤" means "is less than or equal to."

### Minus

The origin of the minus symbol is unclear, although the mathematical concept of subtraction was well known to the ancient Egyptians and appeared in the Rhind papyrus among others. The word *minus* was used by the Romans in a generalized sense, and it was not until the great mathematician Fibonacci published his works in 1202 that it was clearly defined as an algebraic operation. The symbol may have been derived from shorthand notation, but was possibly specified for the first time in the works of John Widmann, dated 1489.

### Multiplication

The modern symbol for multiplication appears to have been first used in printed form by the famous English mathematician William Oughtred (1574–1660), and was included in several of his treatises including the *Clavis Mathematicae,* which was published in Latin in 1631. Another famous mathematician, Leibniz, objected to the use of the cross to represent multiplication, as he thought it was too easy to mix up with the letter *x.* He used a simple dot instead, a convention that is still popular to this day.

### N factorial

The factorial of a number is the product of multiplying all the integers between 1 and that number together, so $3! = 6$, and $4! = 24$, and so on. The "n factorial" symbol was originally chosen to help get around the difficulties that printers were having in producing mathematical documents. It was first introduced in 1808 by Christian Kramp of Strassbourg (1760–1826) in order to replace an earlier, more complicated symbol. It is now universally used in algebra.

% + :

### Percentage

The word *percentage* is derived from the Italian words *per cento,* or per hundred. The symbol we are familiar with today has been used since the end of the fifteenth century, although the concept of percentage itself is much older. All goods sold at auction in late Roman times, for instance, had a tax of one hundredth, or one percent, levied on them. In the Middle Ages, especially in Italy, business transactions were often performed using 100 as a common base for financial calculations.

### Plus

The concept of a symbol for addition was known to the ancient Egyptians and was used in their algebra—as found, for instance, in documents known as the "Rhind papyrus" and the "Ahmes papyrus" (c. 1550 B.C.). The modern symbol for addition seems to have been first used in a book on arithmetic by Johann Widman, which was published in Leipzig in 1489. It was not generally accepted at the time, and the symbol still needed explanation in the seventeenth century: in 1672, an English mathematician named Hodder wrote "note that a + sign doth signifie Addition."

### Ratio

The symbol for ratio refers to relative amounts, and is therefore also used to represent proportion. It is thought to have been first used in England in the early seventeenth century, where it was printed in a book titled *Johnson's Arithmetick: In Two Bookes,* which was published in London in 1633. In this work the ratio symbol was used to indicate a fraction, three quarters being written 3:4. In 1651, an astronomical publication written by Vincent Wing called *Harmonicon Coeleste* used the ratio symbol in the way we use it today.

### Similar

The symbol that means "is similar to" was probably first used by the famous mathematician Leibniz (1646–1716). He made many important contributions to the subject of mathematical symbolism, and used this sign in statements to show that two or more terms were similar in quantity.

### Square root

The square root symbol used to be called the "radical," and has changed often since ancient times. Late medieval Latin writers used the letter *R*, an abbreviation for the word *radix*. The early Arab mathematicians used various symbols for expressing a root, although the Europeans didn't make use of them. The symbol used today first appeared in print in 1525, although it was not generally accepted until the seventeenth century.

### Summation sign

The Greek letter sigma is used to represent an act of summation. This notation was first used by Leonhard Euler (1707–1783), a Swiss scientist who was also the most prolific mathematician who ever lived. While sigma can be used to mean simple addition, it is generally used in more complex mathematical situations to indicate a summation between certain specified limits.

### Universal quantifier

The universal quantifier is another symbol used in predicate logic to make an assertion within a statement. Together with the existential quantifier, it covers the vast majority of logical operations performed in mathematics. It takes a variable and a formula, and asserts that the given formula holds true for a specified set of values.

### Zero

While numbers have been found recorded on bones by Palaeolithic people dating back over 30,000 years, it was not until advanced civilizations came about that a symbol for zero was invented. Although the Babylonians were fairly advanced mathematicians, they did not seem to use the zero concept; instead they used a space. It appears that several cultures started to use a zero symbol at more or less the same time, one being the Hindu civilization of the Indian subcontinent. By the time of the ancient Greeks, zero symbols were being regularly used in many parts of the world, including by the Mayas of Central and South America.

# Modern Information Symbols

The development of many modern information symbols have followed the globalization and spread of technology and modern conveniences. Much time, energy, and thought has gone into devising clear explanatory symbols whose meaning is obvious whatever the language of the viewer. Hence danger symbols warn clearly of possible (or probable) harm to life and limb and they can be easily interpreted whatever language the viewer speaks. More prosaic symbols also have their uses, such as those shown on fabrics giving washing and cleaning information; on food packaging giving storage, heating, and eating requirements; and electrical goods showing vital information pertaining to safe usage. Not all modern symbols are international — though there is a growing tendency for them to become so. Most continents have their own mapping, road use, and weather symbols, many of which are self-explanatory.

It seems that every modern company, corporation, and association in the world has a symbol, which is often also their logo or trademark. This is frequently made up of the letters of the company name but can also allude to the nature of its work or product. Such symbols become international as the company expands and in time needs no accompanying words to explain the product it represents. Thus athletes can wear the logo of a company and promote its image without the necessity of using words of any language. Multinationals, in particular, take great pains with their logo, and punitive laws protect and restrict its use. This type of symbol is beyond the scope of this book, but this use of symbols is perhaps the most pertinent modern development of their long and distinguished history.

### Amphetamines/dangerous drugs

This symbol is used on bottle labels and on information in the medical profession to warn of dangerous drugs, particularly amphetamines. Drugs like these are administered by physicians with great caution for the treatment of extreme conditions such as narcolepsy. Their use is legally restricted, since they are addictive and can lead to severe mental health problems. Amphetamines are, however, used recreationally (and illegally)—they are a powerful central nervous system stimulant.

### Atom

This is the symbol for an atom, which is defined as the smallest part of an element that can exist independently. An atom consists of a tiny central nucleus surrounded by electrons, protons, and neutrons. The number of electrons and protons contained within the atom determines the element's properties. This symbol is used to indicate nuclear power in general as well as an atom in particular.

### Biological hazard warning

Organisms or products of organisms that present a threat to human health are regarded as biological hazards, or biohazards. This warning sign is shown on equipment, containers, workplaces, materials, and even around animals that may be contaminated with infectious agents. In particular the symbol is used to warn of the hazardous nature of the contents when dangerous liquids or substances are being transported or stored. The symbol was originally an American sign but has become international as its relevance has become more ubiquitous.

### Corrosive

This hazard identification sign indicates that the substance is corrosive to the skin or eyes or can cause chemical burns. The substance can be either an acid or an alkali. The sign should also identify the substance to provide more information on the severity of the hazard. Strict regulations govern the storage, handling, and safe transportation of corrosive substances. Corrosives are used in a wide variety of industries, and include some pesticides and everyday products such as bleaches.

### Flammable material

Flammable materials in the workplace, in public places, or in transit are marked with this hazard identification sign. They are classified as materials liable to: burn at relatively low temperatures; burst into flame spontaneously on contact with air; release a flammable gas on contact with water; cause a fire when exposed to heat, sparks, or flames, or as a result of friction. The substance should also be clearly labeled so that it can be handled, stored, or transported in such a way as to minimize the dangers of flammability. The sign also warns the emergency services that the substance requires special handling during an incident.

### High voltage

This sign is displayed on all high-voltage sources— including electrical equipment, capacitors, battery banks, and electricity substations—to warn of the potential danger. High-voltage cables, whether underground or above ground, can also be a potential hazard to workers or people in the vicinity and are clearly marked with the hazard identification sign. Strict guidelines govern how close public contractors can work near high-voltage sources, as the current can arc to nearby equipment. High-voltage electricity can cause both burns and electrocution.

  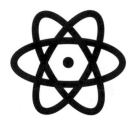

### Laser beam

The word *laser* is an acronym for "light amplification by stimulated emission of radiation." Lasers have a variety of uses in both industrial processes and health care. However, there are dangers inherent in the use of lasers: the concentrated light beam can produce cuts and lesions or damage eyesight, and the laser equipment emits hazardous substances including fumes caused by materials interacting with the beam. Protective measures include wearing eye protectors, masks, and protective clothing. There can also be a danger of fire from lasers.

### Non-ionizing radiation

This hazard identification sign has to be displayed in all workplaces where this form of radiation occurs at levels where there may be a health danger. Non-ionizing radiation is caused by optical radiation and electromagnetic fields. There are guidelines concerning the maximum amount of non-ionizing radiation a person should be exposed to. A number of industrial processes, as well as electrical equipment, telecommunications, lasers, welding equipment, and electricity supply, can cause non-ionizing radiation.

### Nuclear power

This symbol shows diagrammatically the elliptical path that an electron takes when orbiting a nucleus in an atom. The symbol itself is used in connection with all things nuclear, including research, physics, and nuclear reactors. Nuclear power (or fission) is created by splitting a heavy atomic nucleus into two approximately equal portions, which causes the release of energy and free neutrons. Nuclear power and atomic bombs are created by fission in uranium and plutonium.

### Radiation

Ionizing radiation is a hazard in workplaces containing either radioactive materials or machines producing ionizing radiation. Regulations determine the safe dosage of radioactivity to which the worker can be exposed and personal protective measures include shields and special clothing. Ionizing radiation health effects are somatic (affecting the body tissue, which can have an immediate or long-term effect) and genetic (affecting the body's hereditary material). Common sources of radiation are X rays, the nuclear processing industry, luminous paints, and electronic devices using high accelerating voltages and beam currents.

### Risk of explosion

This universal hazard identification sign identifies a risk of explosion. Substances stored or handled in the workplace, or transported, have to be labeled with this sign, so that all who come into contact with them can take appropriate precautions or, in the event of a potentially dangerous incident, emergency services can be clearly warned of potential dangers. Explosive substances include solids, gases, and chemicals and have a wide variety of uses, including those used in industries such as construction and mining.

### Smiley face

The yellow smiley sign appeared for the first time in the 1960s as a counterculture symbol showing that drugs could be bought and used where the sign was seen. Once the meaning became generally known its usage declined almost completely until it started to be used again in the later decades of the twentieth century. It was commonly used in drug culture as a symbol for LSD (lysergic acid diethylamide) or "acid," the psychedelic drug of choice for many in the late 1960s and 1970s. In the 1980s the sign came to symbolize the rave drug Ecstasy.

### Strong magnetic field

Although our common environment has a magnetic field, excessive exposure to a strong magnetic field can be detrimental to health. The hazard identification sign for a strong magnetic field must be displayed in places where this occurs. Industries dealing with or generating large quantities of metals or electricity are most at risk, but also users of some electrical equipment can be exposed to a strong magnetic field.

### Toxic hazard

A toxic substance is one that causes damages to cells or tissue through swallowing, inhalation, or skin contact. There is a wide range of toxic hazards, and they are not necessarily hazardous only for humans but also for the wider environment. The danger can range from low toxicity, where recovery after exposure is usual, to high toxicity, which can cause permanent injury or even be fatal. Toxic materials are used in a variety of industrial processes, and also include pesticides.

### Weak stimulants

This medical symbol warns of medicine containing weak stimulants. Many medical conditions require the administration of mildly stimulating drugs, but even these must be administered with caution depending on the age and condition of the patient. Two commonly taken weak stimulants used to uplift flagging spirits and to keep oneself awake when tired are tea and coffee, both of which contain an alkaloid called caffeine. Caffeine is a weak stimulant of the central nervous system.

### Female

The symbol for the female gender is represented by the symbol for the mythological goddess Venus, which depicts a maiden with a mirror; it is composed of the cross of spirit under the circle of life. As the Roman goddess of love and beauty, she symbolizes love, peace, appreciation of beauty, and harmony in relationships. She also represents the possibility of becoming self-indulgent and overly fond of luxury and comfort. This symbol is also used for the planet Venus.

### Male

The symbol for the male gender is represented by the same symbol used for the planet and mythological god Mars: a warrior with an arrow. Mars represents the masculine properties of energy, ambition, initiative, and courage under adverse conditions. Known to the ancients as the god of war, Mars is often associated with physical violence or the desire to conquer one's goals. However, Mars is also known as the god of husbandry, and as such represents a love of nature. This is used widely as a sign, from such diverse places as scientific documents to public toilets.

### Female-female

The symbol for lesbian women is usually made up of two superimposed female gender signs, and while this has been used since the 1970s to denote gay women, it has also been used by some to represent feminist or "sisterhood of women" movements. It is sometimes referred to as "the mirror of Venus." A modified version of the symbol has also sometimes been used by feminist lesbians via the addition of a third female gender sign to indicate a rejection of the concept of monogamy, which they viewed as a male imposition.

**Modern Information Symbols**

### Male-male

The symbol for homosexual men is made up of two superimposed male gender signs, and has been used since the 1970s to denote gay men. It is sometimes known as the "double mars" or "double man" sign. It is used for many purposes, including on signs to indicate establishments that welcome gay men. The symbol for a transgender person is sometimes created from superimposed male and female symbols, such that the arrow and the cross join on the same ring.

### At

When bookkeeping and accounts were all painstakingly handwritten, this symbol was used to show how many items at a certain price were recorded. But the symbol became increasingly redundant in the computer age, as automatic systems made auditing quicker. However, this symbol had a complete resurgence with the arrival of the Internet, and it has now become an indispensable part of e-mail addresses. The symbol is now seen used in its own right as a general indication of all matters pertaining to the Internet.

### Copyright

This symbol is used to indicate that a given work, intellectual property, or image must not be used without the permission of the owner of the copyright. Copyright protection extends over literature, drama, art works, recordings, film, and many other areas. The laws pertaining to copyright vary from country to country as well as in how the "work" is commissioned, paid for, and originated. However, the right to a copyright can be bought and sold in the same way as any goods.

### Made from recycled material

The symbol that indicates that some or all of a product has been made from recycled material is composed of the three "recycle" arrows on a black circular background. Sometimes there will be a number shown between the arrows—this indicates the percentage of the product that has been made from recycled materials. This symbol is most commonly seen on containers and packaging, and may be accompanied with a message such as "Printed on recycled paper."

### Recycle symbol

The symbol used to represent "recycle" is derived from three arrows arranged in a circular manner such that there is no beginning and no end. There are two main forms of this sign: the arrows may be black or as shown here, in outline only. It is used on materials that can be recycled, often with a message stating "This product can be recycled" or "Recyclable." The extent to which this can be done may be limited by local regulations or resources.

### Registered trademark

This ubiquitous symbol shows that a particular word, phrase, logo, or any distinctive identification mark or design enjoys restricted use by the owners, who can defend their right to its use through the law. It distinguishes the owner's goods and services from all others by appearing on its products and packaging. This guarantees the consumer that they are buying authenticated goods from the designated company. This right is enforceable through the law if companies are careful to guard their identity; they will often pursue anyone they consider to be infringing on their rights.

### Bass clef

This musical notation symbol indicates the bass melody. It is placed on the fourth line of a staff (also called a stave) on the left side of the music to show that the notes it indicates start at the next F note after middle C. Musical notation was developed in the thirteenth century as a way of permanently recording the new and more complex musical arrangements that were being composed.

### Treble clef

Also called the violin clef. This symbol shows the musician the higher notes from the G above middle C. It is placed on the second line of the staff at the left-hand side of the music. The staff on which the notation is written is a set of five parallel horizontal lines with four spaces between them. This is a development of a medieval system for recording plainchant—until then only the pitch, not the length, of the notes was indicated.

### Quarter note

Also called a crotchet. This symbol tells the musician how long to hold the note before moving to the next. Also, its place on the notation grid indicates which key it should be played in. There are nine different notes, in order of duration starting with the longest: long breve, breve, whole note (also called a semibreve), half note (or minim), quarter note (or crotchet), eighth note (or quaver), 16th note (or semiquaver), 32nd note (demisemiquaver), and 64th note (hemidemisemiquaver).

### Blowing snow

This symbol forecasts difficult and even dangerous driving conditions when blowing snow can obscure visibility completely. Once snow has fallen, conditions can be clear and visibility excellent; however, if the snow is not frozen into place, strong gusts of wind can whip up snow flakes or powder creating complete white-out conditions.

### Calm winds

A double hollow circle signifies calm winds. This is defined as having a wind speed of less than 1 mph or Force 0 on the Beaufort scale. At sea this indicates dead calm. The Beaufort scale originally read from 0 to 12 (hurricane strength) and was devised by Rear Admiral Sir Francis Beaufort (1774–1857) for use at sea. In 1926 it was modified to show wind speeds on land; it was further modified in 1955 by the U.S. Weather Bureau to read up to level 17, but the upper levels are very extreme wind conditions and rarely reached.

### Dust

Dust consists of minute particles of solid matter in the atmosphere that can be blown around the world on the winds. Dust is drawn up into the atmosphere by dry winds blowing over desert regions or areas of arid loose soil; by human activity through crop and forest burning; and as a by-product of burning fossil fuels. It is also expelled into the upper atmosphere during volcanic explosions. Visibility can be badly affected and allergy and asthma sufferers can be seriously affected by breathing such polluted air.

### Fog

Fog is defined as cloud located in the lower atmosphere that reduces visibility to less than half a mile. Fog is made up of a thick mass of water droplets and differs from mist by the size and density of the water droplets—visibility is better in mist conditions. Fog often forms in fall and winter when the earth's surface cools under a cloudless night sky; the fog persists for some hours after daybreak and has generally dispersed by early afternoon. In some conditions—such as forest burning and factory fumes—fog can be made up of smoke and dust particles; in such cases the fog can persist for days.

### Haze

Haze is mostly created by pollution and is defined as tiny solid smoke or dust particles that reduce visibility to between 0.6 and 1.25 miles. Typically it has a yellowish-brown hue or a bluish tinge. Haze can occur in urban areas when conditions are particularly calm and there is no wind to disperse dust and smoke particles. The conditions also require a temperature inversion—this is a zone in which the temperature increases with altitude rather than, as usual, declines. Haze conditions can be dangerous for people who suffer from allergies or asthma.

### Heavy snow

Snow is precipitation formed when the temperature of water vapor in the atmosphere drops below freezing point and ice crystals coalesce to form flakes. Meteorologists forecast snow in three forms: light, moderate, and heavy. Shown here is the symbol for heavy snow, consisting of four crosses (two crosses show light snow, three show moderate). The size of snowflakes depends on the amount of water vapor and the temperature. Snowflakes are larger in warmer temperatures and small when there are low concentrations of water vapor.

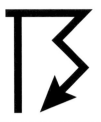

### Heavy thunderstorm

A thunderstorm is a short-lived weather system that affects a localized area. Characteristically heavy rain, strong winds, thunder, and lightning occur. There are symbols for both light and heavy thunderstorms: for light thunderstorms the jagged arrow points down and right, while for heavy it points down and left. Thunderstorms form in three stages: immaturity, maturity, and decay. During the immature stage, warm air rises and clouds start to form vertically (over 30,000 ft.) and horizontally (6–9 miles) and begin to form cumulonimbus clouds. At maturity the strong updraft weakens and water droplets in the cloud start to fall, creating a downdraft.

### Ice pellets

This is the term used for frozen rain droplets that are made up of ice crystals of varying degrees of hardness and have a diameter of less than .02 in. (0.5 mm). This condition is more commonly known as sleet. The condition occurs when rain falls through a relatively mild temperature layer of air and then descends through a deep layer of much colder air, which freezes the rain into crystals before they hit the ground.

### Lightning

The symbol for lightning is a jagged arrow pointing down and right. Lightning occurs when violent ascending air currents—such as those in cumulonimbus cloud—act within a cloud to separate positive charges upward and the negative charges downward. The cloud then affects the ground below it so that the ground becomes positively charged. When the natural resistance of the air is overwhelmed by the strength of the charges in the cloud and in the ground, lightning is produced. The two main types of lightning are fork lightning and sheet lighting.

### Light freezing rain

Freezing rain happens when rain from a mild air layer descends through a layer of freezing air; meteorologically it is termed either light or moderate. The symbol for moderate freezing rain has another hollow square in the right bend. The rain becomes supercooled to such a degree that when it reaches the ground it freezes on contact, leaving a crust of ice. When the rain droplets are smaller than .02 in. (0.5 mm) in diameter, the conditions are termed "freezing drizzle." The symbols for freezing and moderate freezing drizzle are the same as for freezing rain, except the square has an extended right edge.

### Light rain

Rain is divided into three types: light, moderate, and heavy. Shown here are two small hollow squares that signify light rain (three squares are for moderate, four for heavy). Rain is defined as the type of precipitation falling in water droplets larger than .02 in. (.5 mm) and consisting of droplets that condense in the atmosphere, grow in size and weight to form clouds, and then individually fall to earth.

### Light snow showers

Snow showers occur as light or moderate; the symbol is differentiated by an extra line within the triangle for moderate snow showers. Snow showers generally indicate unstable weather conditions before a system sets in for a period. They tend to be short-lived and localized and can anticipate snowfall.

### Moderate drizzle

Drizzle is defined as being precipitation falling in water droplets smaller than .02 in. (0.5 mm). Drizzle is divided into three types: light, moderate, and heavy. Shown here are three hollow squares with an extended line indicating moderate drizzle. Two squares forecast light drizzle and four squares heavy. The three classifications show the degree of visibility: in light drizzle objects are visible at distances of over 1,100 yards; in medium drizzle objects are visible between 550 and 1,100 yards; and in heavy drizzle objects can only be seen to a maximum of 550 yards.

### ⅞ths cloud cover

There are various degrees of cloud cover defined by meteorologists for weather maps. The symbol starts as a hollow circle that is filled in depending on the amount of cloud cover. ⅞ths cloud cover is almost total, so the symbol is almost entirely filled in. There are three distinct types of cloud: cirrus, cumulus, and stratus; and four distinct altitude groups: low clouds, middle clouds, high clouds, and vertical clouds, which can encompass any of the groups.

### Snow grains

This is a type of frozen precipitation made up of white ice grains that have a diameter of under .04 in. (1 mm). They are usually produced by minute precipitation falling through cold air from stratus and stratocumulus clouds. The effect is a type of icy drizzle that can be light, medium, or heavy and similarly affect visibility. Objects are visible in light conditions over 1,100 yards; medium gives visibility at 550 to 1,100 yards; and heavy restricts visibility to below 550 yards.

 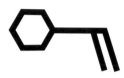

### Tropical hurricane

Hurricanes start as a group of violent thunderstorms over tropical oceans near the equator, which take their energy from the warm waters. A zone of low pressure develops in the center, and as the system develops, the winds gather speed, the pressure in the middle drops even further, and the system starts to spin away from the equator. When wind speeds reach 39 mph it becomes a tropical storm (the symbol is the same except the central disk is hollow) and is given a code name. When winds reach 73 mph it becomes a hurricane. The Saffir-Simpson Hurricane Intensity Scale grades hurricanes into five levels, with five being the most destructive.

### Winds of 18–22 knots

Wind strength is differentiated on weather maps to indicate direction and strength. The basic symbol is a hollow hexagon with a horizontal line indicating wind speed of less than 3 knots. As the wind strength increases, the number of lines branching off the horizontal line increase; these also point in the direction that the wind is coming from; in this case, it is an east wind.

# Bibliography

Bottomley, Frank, *The Church Explorer's Guide to Symbols and Their Meaning*, Kaye & Ward, London, 1978.

Bulfinch, Thomas, *Bulfinch's Mythology*, Dell Publishing Co., Inc, New York, 1967.

Carlyon, Richard, *A Guide to the Gods*, William Heinemann Ltd, London, 1981.

Clayton, Peter A., *Chronicle of the Pharaohs*, Thames and Hudson Ltd, London, 1994.

Cooper, J. C., *An Illustrated Encyclopaedia of Traditional Symbols*, Thames and Hudson Ltd, London, 1978.

Hall, James, *Hall's Illustrated Dictionary of Symbols in Eastern and Western Art*, John Murray (Publishers) Ltd, London, 1994.

Hooker, J. T., *Reading the Past*, British Museum Press, London, 1990.

Lewis, Philippa & Gillian Darley, *Dictionary of Ornament*, Macmillan London Limited, 1986.

Lurker, Manfred, *The Gods and Symbols of Ancient Egypt*, Thames and Hudson Ltd, London, 1980.

Mitchell, A. G., *Hindu Gods and Goddesses*, Her Majesty's Stationery Office, London, 1982.

Oates, Joan, *Babylon*, Thames and Hudson, London, 1979.

Polakoff, Claire, *African Textiles and Dyeing Techniques*, Routledge & Kegan Paul, London, 1982.

Savill, Sheila and Elizabeth Locke, *Pears Encyclopaedia of Myths and Legends, Ancient Near and Middle East, Ancient Greece and Rome*, Pelham Books Ltd, 1976.

Savill, Sheila, *Pears Encyclopaedia of Myths and Legends, The Orient*, Pelham Books Ltd, 1977.

# Index

A, Buddhist 54
aban 39
abundance 166
Acacia 25
acorn 157
Adinkra 38–52
Adinkrahene 39
Adwo 39
Aegricanes 101
African 38–52, 60
air 204
Akoben 40
Akokonan 40
Akoma 40
Akoma ntoso 41
albatross 136
alchemy 204–217
alcohol town 176
alertness 166
Algiz 74
All-seeing eye 11
aluminum 193
amalgam 206
amentet 17
amphetamines 238
amun 17
anarchy 126
anarchy, German 127
anchor 146
ancient sun sign 78
anemone 157
anhur 18
Ankh 11
annual 218
Ansuz 71
antelope 25
Anti-ANC South African 126
antimony 193
anuket 18

apocalypse 109
apocalyptic lamb 109
apple 157
aqua fortis 206
aqua regia 206
Aquarius 84 .
Aries 81
armed and hostile man 176
arsenic 194
Asase ye dur 41
Ashanti 38–52
ass 137
Assyrian sun god 26
astrology 80–88
at 244
atom 238
Aum 54
aurora borealis 226
Aya 41

baboon 26
bane/deadly 90
basilisk 137
bass clef 246
Bat 54
battle 147
bay tree 158
beard 147
bee 137
bell 55
Berkana 75
beware—crime scene 177
beware of thieves 178
biennial 218
Bin nka bi 42
biological hazard 238
birch tree 158
bird 15
bismuth 194

bleeding heart 109
blessing 90
Blood of Isis 18
blowing snow 247
boar 88, 101
book 11
borax 207
bright prospects 166
brimstone 207
Britannia 134
Buddhist 54, 55, 57, 58, 59,
   60, 63, 66, 67, 68, 85, 120
buffalo 55
bulcranium 101
bull 138
bush 218
business symbols 244–245
butterfly 55
Byzantine emperors sign 131

caduceus 102
calm winds 247
Cancer 82
candle 147
Canterbury 117
Capricorn 84
captivity 167
caput mortuum 207
carbon 195
carnation 158
carp 56
caryatid 102
cat 26
caution—judge lives here 178
cedar 27
Celtic 118
centaur 102
Ceres 227

chains 148
cherry 56
cherub 148
chief 167
China 7, 8, 28, 34, 53, 54,
   55, 56, 57, 58, 59, 60,
   62, 63, 64, 65, 66, 67,
   68, 78, 97
Chinese astrology 80, 85–88
Cho Ku Rei 91
chrismon 110
Christian fish 110
Christian symbol for fish 110
chrysanthemum 56
cicada 57
cinnabar 208
cloud 57
club 57
cobalt 195
cock 58
comedy mask 148
consecrated church 118
copper 196
coptic cross 118
copyright 244
corn 27
cornucopia see horn of plenty
corrosive 239
courthouse in town 178
cow 27
coyote tracks 167
crane 138
crescent 28
crocodile 28
cross four-fs 119
crosses 117–124
crow 58
crown 149
cupid 103

cymbals 149
cypress 28

Dagaz 77
dagger 58
Dame-dame 42
danger 179
danger—be alert 179
danger—don't drink the
   water 179
dangerous dog lives here 180
date palm 29
deadly 219
defiance 168
Democrat donkey 126
desert 12
determinatives 10
dioecious 219
division 230
dog 88, 138
dog of Fo 59
dolphin 139
Donnerkeil/thunderbolt 127
doom 111
door 111
double crown 19
dove 139
dove of peace 139
dragon 8, 59, 86
dragonfly 59
drum 60
duck 140
dust 247
dwarf 134
Dwennimmen 42

eagle 140
eagle and serpent 140
eagle, American 136

eagle, double-headed 127
eagle, imperial 128
eagle, Nazi German 129
earth 91, 205, 223
Eastern star 29
Eastern symbols 53–68
eat 12
egg 159
Egyptian 7, 8, 10–37, 38, 81, 82, 94, 97, 111
Ehwaz 76
Eihwaz 74
elements 193–203
elephant 60
elf cross 78
enclosure for ceremonial dance 168
Epa 43
Ese Ne Tekrema 43
essential oil 208
everlasting life 168
existential quantifier 230
Eye of Horus 12

falcon 29
fall 89
fasces 150
feather 150
Fehu 70
female 243
female-female 243
fertility 91
fig 159
Fihankra 43
finite difference or increment 230
fire 6, 150, 204
five sacred wounds 111
flail 30
flammable material 239
fleur-de-lis 151
ficuree 119
fly 30
fofoo 44
fog 248
force 13
four ages of man 169
fox 141
free food 180
free handouts to go 180
free medical help 181
free phone call 181
Freemasons 11
friendship 92, 169
frog 30
fu 60

funtunfunefu denkyemfunefu 44

Gebo 72
Gemini 81
glass 208
globical 119
Gnostic sun 112
go the other way 181
goat 87
God 13, 92
Goddess 92
gohei 61
gold 196
good campsite 182
good omen 169
good potential here 182
good prospects 170
good railroad jump point 182
good road 183
goose 61
gorgon 103
gourd 61
graffiti, Serbian 131
grail 151
grapevine 159
grasshopper 141
Greek letter omega 231
Greek letter pi 231
Greek letter theta 231
Green Man 134
griffin 141
guarding 170
guidance 170
Gye Nyame 44

Hagalaz 72
hare 86
harp 151
Hathor 19
hawthorn 160
haze 248
hazel 160
healing and health 93
heart 152
heavy snow 248
heavy thunderstorm 249
helmet 152
hermatite 209
hieroglyphics 7, 10–37
Hindu 54, 55, 57, 58, 60, 61, 66, 117
hippopotamus 31
ho-ho bird 62

holly 160
Hon Sha Ze Sho Nen 93
horn of plenty 152
horse 87, 142, 170
horseshoe 153
hostile cops 183
hostile laws and locals 183
hourglass 153
house 13
house temporarily empty 184
Hwemudua 45
hydrogen 197
Hye Wonhye 45

ice pellets 249
ideograms 10, 14
India 28, 53
infinite number of petals 219
infinity 232
Ingwuz 77
integral sign 232
Iona 120
iron 197
Iron Cross 128
is less than or equal to 232
Isa 73
Isis 19
Islam 28, 46
ivy 161

jail 184
Japan 28, 53, 54, 55, 56, 57, 58, 59, 61, 62, 63, 65, 67
Jera 73
Jerusalem 120
Jewish 112, 113, 116
journey 170
Juno 227
Jupiter 224
Jupiter's staff 103
justice 8, 104

K'ayab 79
keep moving 184
Kenaz 71
Khnum 20
Khons 20
kind man here 185
kind woman here 185
kintinkantan 45
knot 153
kolowi 46
kramo-bone amma

yanhu kram-pa 46
Ku Klux Klan 129
kuronti ne akwamu 46

Laguz 76
lamb 112
lamb and flag 112
lamp 31
laser beam 240
Latin 121
lawman's house 185
lead 198
leading to happiness 170
League of Arab States 129
lechery 113
Leo 82
liberty 135
Libra 83
light freezing rain 250
light rain 250
light snow showers 250
lighthearted 172
lightning 249
lily 161
lion 135
litharge 209
logogram indicator 14
Lotus 31
love 9, 93
Lower Egypt 20
lyre 104

Maat 21
made from recycled material 245
magic circle 94
magical energy 94
magnesium 198
magnolia 62
magpie 62
make Bible talk 186
male 243
male-male 244
Maltese 121
man 14, 172
mandala 63
Mannaz 76
marcasite 209
Marianne 135
marriage 94
Mars 223
mathematical symbols 230–236
Mayan 79
Menorah 113
Mercury 199, 210, 222

mermaid 142
Meshkhent 21
mineral kingdom 220
minus 233
mistletoe 161
Mmusuyidee 47
moderate drizzle 251
monkey 87, 142
Monogram of Jesus 113
Moon 228
move on186
mpuannum 47
multiplication 233
music 246
mystical symbols 89–100
mythical symbols 101–107

n factorial 233
Narcissus 63
Native Americans 7
Native American symbols 78, 166–176
Nauthiz 73
Nazi 69, 126
Nazi SS runes 130
Nazi swastika 130
Neith 21
Nekhbet 22
Neptune 225
net 32
niter 210
nitrogen 199
nkonsonkonson 47
nkyinkyim 48
noisy dog 186
non-ionizing radiation 240
Norse 69–77, 104, 105
nsaa 48
nsoromma 48
nuclear power 240
Nut 22
Nyame Birbi Wo Soro 49
Nyame Nnwu Na Mawu 49

obelisk 32
octogram 32
Odenkyem 49
Odin's cross 104
Odin's staff 105
Odo Nnyew Fie Kwan 50
ohene adwa 50
oil 210
oil of vitriol 211
OK 187
olive 162
olive oil 211

255

**Index**

orange 63
origins of the universe 64
orpiment 211
Osiris 22
osram ne nsromma 50
osrane 51
Othala 77
ounce 212
ourobouros 95
owl 143
owo foro adobe 51
ox 85
oxygen 200

pagan 80, 94
paintbrush 64
Pallas 228
palm 33
papal 121
papyrus 33
patee 122
patee formee 122
paths crossing 172
patriarchal 122
peace 95, 130, 173
peach 64
peacock 143
pelican 114
pentacle 95
pentagram 96
peony 65
percentage 234
perennial 220
pernicious 220
Pertho 74
Philosopher's stone 96
phoenix 33
phonograms 10, 14
phosphorus 200
physical and magical
    strength 96
pictograms 7
pine tree 65
pineapple 162
Pisces 84
planets 222–226
platinum 201
plentiful crops 173
plenty game 173
plum 65
plural indicator 14
plus 234
Pluto 226
poisonous 221
pomegranate 34
Pop 79

poppy 162
potassium 201
precipitation 212
protection 174
psychic awareness 97
purification 97

quarter note 246
quicklime 212

radiation 241
Raido 71
rat 85
ratio 234
realgar 213
rebirth 97
recycle symbol 245
registered trademark 245
Reiki 91, 92, 97
Republican elephant 131
Reshef 23
rhinoceros 66
risk of explosion 241
rod of Aesculpius 105
Roman sacred cross 123
rooster 88
rose 163
Russian Orthodox 123

sad story will get you food
    187
safe place/clean water 187
Sagittarius 83
sal ammoniac 213
salamander 143
salt 213
saltpeper 214
sankofa 51
Satis 23
Saturn 224
satyr 105
say nothing 188
scallop shell 114
scarab 34
Scorpio 83
scruple 214
scythe 154
seal of the world 114
Sebek 23
secure and protected 188
Sei He Ki 98
Sekhmet 24
serpent 144
Seshat 24
/ths cloud cover 251
sex signs 243–244

shamash 34
shou 66
sickle 154
sign of the desert 174
signum dei 115
silence 188
silver 202
similar 235
skull 154
skull and crossbones 155
small 15
smiley face 241
snake 86
snow grains 251
sodium 202
solar barque 35
solar bodies 222–229
someone here 189
Sowilo 75
sphinx 35
spider 98
spirit 214
spiritually 98
spring 89
square root 235
squatter sign, German
    128
St. Andrew's 123
St. John 115
St. Luke 115
St. Mark 116
St. Matthew 116
St. Peter's 124
staff of poseidon 106
star 99
Star of David 116
Star of Ishtar 35
steel 215
stop 189
strength 174
strong magnetic field 242
sublimation 215
sulfur 203, 215
summation sign 235
summer 89
sun 6, 15, 99, 229
sun disk 36
sun symbol 175
sunburst 155
sunflower 163
swallow 144
swan 144
swastika 9, 36
swiftness 175
sword 66
sycamore 36

take this direction 189
talc 216
tamfo bebre 52
tartar 216
Tau cross 124
Taurus 81
Teiwaz 75
ten-day week 37
terrestrial globe 155
the blessed sacrament 117
Thor's hammer 106
Three Graces 106
thunderbird 175
Thurisaz 70
tiger 85
tin 203
to rouse jealousy 99
torch 107
tortoise 145
town 15
toxic hazard 242
tragedy mask 149
travel 100
treasure vase 67
treble clef 246
tree 221
tree of life 163
trefly 124
trigram 67
trolley bus stop 190
tropical hurricane 252
tumi te se kosua 52
turtle 78
two seeds of resistance 67

Uncle Sam 136
unicorn 145
universal brotherhood 175
universal quantifier 236
universal seed 216
unsure of this place 190
Upper Egypt 24
Uranus 225
urine 217
urn 156
Uruz 70

Venus 222
Vesta 229
victory 107
viking 104
vinegar 217
Virgo 82
Vishnu 117
Viva! 132
vulture 16

Wadjet 25
walk 16
warding off evil spirits 175
waste of time 190
watch out—troublemaker
    here 191
water 205
water 6
wax 217
wayeb 79
weak stimulants 242
wealthy folk here 191
weather symbols 247–252
weeping willow 164
wheat 164
wheat sheaves 8
wheel 156
wheel of life 68
white power 132
wildlife 136–146
wind 6
windmill 156
winds of 18–22 knots 252
winged disk 37
winged horse 145
winged lion 37
wings 146
winter 90
wise/watchful 176
witch sign 100
woman 16
wood 17, 68, 221
woroso 52
wreath 164
Wunjo 72
wyvern 146

yin and yang 68
yonic 100
you might get attacked
    here 191

zero 236
Zeus 107